To Karyn.
Happy eating!
All the best,

All the best,
Sue Wddd

Tuck in!
Sue

Faith in Food

Faith in Food

Published in 2014 by
Bene Factum Publishing Ltd
PO Box 58122
London
SW8 5WZ
inquiries@bene-factum.co.uk
www.bene-factum.co.uk

FSC
www.fsc.org
MIX
Paper from
responsible sources
FSC® C106600

ISBN: 978-1-909657-41-0
Text © Alliance of Religions and Conservation

A CIP catalogue record of this is available from the British Library.

Book design, typesetting and illustration by Grace Fussell of gracefussellstudio.com
Cover design and illustration by Rosa Vitalie
Printed and bound in Slovenia on behalf of Latitude Press

The opinions expressed in this book are those of the authors and not the Alliance of Religions and Conservation.

Every effort has been made to locate and credit the authors and sources of material reproduced in this publication. In some cases this may not have been possible and no infringement is intended.

Faith in Food

*changing the world
one meal at a time*

Edited by Susie Weldon and Sue Campbell

Bene Factum Publishing

ALLIANCE OF RELIGIONS AND CONSERVATION

launched in 1995 by HRH The Prince Philip, Duke of Edinburgh KG KT

FAITH in FOOD

Changing the world ~
one meal at a time

**NORWEGIAN MINISTRY
OF FOREIGN AFFAIRS**

In memory of my father, John Weldon, a true man of the soil, farmer and food-lover whose prolific vegetable garden taught me the deep satisfaction, deliciousness and hard work involved in growing your own food.

- Susie Weldon

To my husband, Andrew, a would-be farmer, optimistic gardener and cultivator of dreams.

- Sue Campbell

Contents

Acknowledgements

This book would not have been possible without the kindness of strangers. Some of the articles were contributed by 'friends of ARC', such as Patrick Holden of the Sustainable Food Trust, Helen Browning of the Soil Association, and Joyce D'Silva of Compassion in World Farming, who share ARC's vision. However, many of the authors had not heard of ARC before and graciously responded to our requests, which came out of the blue and, no doubt, at an inconvenient time for them. Everyone provided articles or images free of charge, including many of our faith partners, as well as Creative Commons photographers. We are deeply grateful to all our contributors.

We are mindful of the patience shown by Anthony Weldon and Dominic Horsfall at Bene Factum Publishing and their guidance during the process. Special thanks are due to the book's designer Grace Fussell, whose deftness and originality have made a complicated book highly readable, and to Rosa Vitalie for the book's delightful cover.

We are also grateful for the help of the ARC team, in particular Martin Palmer, Victoria Finlay and Tony Benjamin, who contributed articles, proof-read, fact-checked and in every way helped to strengthen this book. Nor would it have been possible without the Royal Ministry of Foreign Affairs, Norway, which supported ARC's Faith in Food initiative.

ARC has produced the book on a not-for-profit basis in order to spark debate and inspire action. Any profits that are generated will go to support faith-based food and farming projects.

The world is waking up to the fact that we have to find ways to produce food more sustainably because of the enormous challenges facing us. With accelerating climate change, rising costs of fuel and fertilizer and a rapidly growing global population, we need to ask whether the way we produce our food is fit for purpose in the very challenging circumstances of the twenty-first century. We simply cannot ignore that question any longer.

The industrialized approach to farming that we have adopted in the past fifty years is pushing the natural world so far that, in some cases, it is struggling to cope. Soils are being disastrously depleted and degraded, demand for water is growing ever more voracious and the entire food production system is at the mercy of an increasingly fluctuating price of oil.

Add to this the catastrophic likelihood of a global temperature rise of 4°C later this century, as stressed in the World Bank report *Turn Down the Heat*, and it is clear that we require a different approach – one that puts Nature and the protection of her ecosystems back at the heart of the whole process. That means taking care of the Earth that sustains us. It means working with Nature and not against her, and it means finding ways to produce more without toxic and artificial fertilizers derived from fossil fuels.

Having myself tried to farm as sustainably as possible for nearly thirty years in England, I have seen at first hand the miraculous ingenuity of Nature. We share this planet with the rest of creation for a very good reason; we cannot exist on our own without the intricately balanced web of life around us. Yet all too many of us have lost a sense of connection with the natural world.

This is where the wisdom and learning offered by the world's sacred traditions is so important. They are custodians of the timeless truth that all life is rooted in our Creator – our Sustainer. The dangerously destructive approach to farming we have adopted in the past fifty years, which signally fails to give back to Nature in return for what we take from her, is contrary to the teachings of each and every one of our major faiths. No agricultural system is truly sustainable unless it also sustains Nature, which is why an agro-ecological approach is so vital.

That is why I am delighted by the publication of *Faith in Food* which offers a timely reminder that food is a sacred gift as well as the means of sustaining our physical life, and that how we obtain that food goes to the heart of our relationship with the natural world and with our Creator. As well as setting out some of the serious challenges facing food and farming today, *Faith in Food* looks at the spiritual significance of food in six major faiths – Buddhism, Christianity, Hinduism, Islam, Judaism and Sikhism – and offers inspiring stories of practical action by faith communities around the world.

Whichever faith tradition we come from, the fact at the heart of the matter is the same. Our inheritance from our Creator is at stake. We have a rapidly narrowing window of opportunity – as individuals, as nations and as an international community – to act with the scale and urgency needed. Our sacred traditions can lead us back into a 'right relationship' with the natural world and restore a sense of reverence for the food that sustains us, the creation that provides it and for the noble profession of farming, the very foundation of a healthy civilization.

Introduction:
'When you eat, you are swallowing the future'

Everyone says the kitchen is the heart of the home. Preparing food for the people we love and eating together is what binds us as friends, family and community. Food is so much at the heart of all that is special and important in our lives, and at the same time so commonplace, that it is easy to forget that eating is also a moral act. Every mouthful we take comes with an invisible trail of impacts: on other people, on animals, on the land and even on ourselves.

Consider this: up to 30% of our individual carbon footprint comes from the food we eat when we calculate the cost of the entire trail

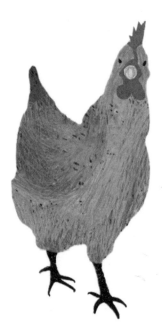

from farm gate to dinner plate, including transport and storage, says Patrick Holden, head of the Sustainable Food Trust. Agriculture influences the way half the world's habitable land is cared for and how two-thirds of its fresh water is used. The industrialisation of farming in recent decades has dramatically boosted crop yields but at huge cost to the environment. All over the world, soil degradation is on the increase. So is water pollution from toxic chemical residues, and so is the devastation of forests chopped down to grow crops (often to feed livestock rather than people).

What's staggering is the speed of the damage; the UN's Food and Agriculture Organization estimates that around three-quarters of the world's genetic diversity of domestic agricultural crops and livestock were lost in the last century.

We must find a way to feed ourselves without trashing the Earth. That's why the Alliance of Religions and Conservation (ARC) launched its **Faith in Food** initiative. ARC was set up in 1995 by HRH The Prince Philip to help the world's major faith groups develop environmental programmes. His view was that as a Christian he felt a personal responsibility to care for God's creation. Surely, he reasoned, people of other faiths would feel the same way. Since then, thousands of faith-based environmental projects have been launched, and every major faith has made caring for the environment a high priority.

But food? While every faith regards food as a gift of the Divine and teaches that we must feed the hungry, it's fair to say that the environmental impact of our food choices is less well understood. Many have never considered these issues — certainly not in the light of their own food provision which can be enormous. Sikh gurdwaras, or temples, feed an estimated 30 million people per day; the New Psalmist Baptist Church in Baltimore, USA, holds 9,000 events a year involving food; many churches serve hot drinks and biscuits after services.

When ARC held a series of four **Faith in Food** workshops in New York, Delhi, Nairobi and London, we heard stories of inspiring action, from faith-run organic farms to schemes linking faith communities to local farmers. We also heard a great many concerns, from the tragedy of 270,000 farmer suicides in India since 1990, to the problem of hunger and the impact of climate change in Africa where, we were told, 'farmers don't know when to plant; the rains don't come when they are supposed to any more'. In New York people spoke of 'urban food deserts' where it is almost impossible to find fresh fruit and vegetables. One participant, from a church with an average attendance of 7,000 worshippers at its Sunday services, said every time the Bishop asks who has high blood pressure or diabetes, hundreds of hands go up.

Uniting the four workshops was a shared sense that something was wrong with the global food system. But the problems were so many and varied that people felt paralysed by the scale of it all. And while some faith groups were very active in this area, many others didn't really understand the issues and wanted help as they navigated their way through the sustainable food and farming maze.

That's the reason for this book. It offers a buffet menu of articles on some of the key issues, many of them written by a wide variety of eminent contributors, alongside inspiring stories of faith action on food and farming. Throughout we have seasoned it with beautiful food prayers and blessings from the six faiths highlighted here: Buddhism, Christianity, Hinduism, Judaism, Islam and Sikhism. We have also looked at the spiritual significance of food, with personal viewpoints from members of each of these faiths. Finally, we have tips for action to make the food we grow, buy and eat more sustainable.

The book is subtitled *'Changing the world one meal at the time'* because we profoundly believe that through building a new relationship with our food based on our beliefs and values, we can transform the global food system for the better. In fact we must: our survival depends on a healthy planet, especially if we are to meet the needs of a rapidly growing global population.

We are very aware, however, that for some families struggling to put food — any food — on the table, whether it is sustainable or not, may seem an irrelevant luxury. As one participant at our New York workshop said: 'I'm trying to think what I'd say to someone who's dealing with 'roaches and rats in their home.'

That's why our message is 'one meal at a time'. All contributions, no matter how seemingly small and insignificant, make a difference. Consuming more fresh vegetables, or cooking from scratch, or growing our own herbs, or eating seasonally, or walking to the shops instead of driving, or buying fairly traded food or free-range eggs: each is a vote for a healthier, more sustainable food and farming system that has the added advantage of a healthier, more sustainable us.

And these daily votes really do make a difference, as sixth-generation American farmer Harry Stoddart says in his book *Real Dirt: An Ex-Industrial Farmer's Guide to Sustainable Eating*: 'You, as an eater, have more power over the food system than governments or multi-national corporations because collectively, eaters spend more than either.

Significantly more.' Harry adds: 'When you eat, you are swallowing the future — literally and figuratively. Current agricultural practices are diminishing our ability to produce food in the future. Hence…your food choices today will influence what is produced in the future.'

This book is not meant to be the final word on these massive issues but the beginning of a conversation that will, we hope, help us all rediscover a sense of the sacred in food.

The ecological crisis is as much a crisis of the spirit as of the Earth; it is high time we rediscovered a true appreciation for the gift of food we receive each day.

After all, if we are what we eat, it is worth remembering the words of the ancient Hindu text, the **Chandogya Upanishad**:

'When one's food is pure, one's being becomes pure.'

Susie Weldon and Sue Campbell,
January 2014

Agriculture:
The Farmers' Tales

"One of the
greatest opportunities
to live our values
— or betray them —
lies in the food we
put on our plates."

– *Jonathan Safran Foer, American writer*

Reflection on Soil

"And the Lord God formed a man of the dust of the ground, and breathed into his nostrils the breath of life; and the man became a living being"

– Genesis 2:7

Soils are a puzzling act: groundlessly un-noticeable but heavenly crucial. The Book of Genesis in the Bible is a powerful reminder. When it describes God creating humans out of dirt, we are reminded of our humble origins.

This is still true for modern men and women. We are what we eat, and it is not a joke. We have inside our bodies the element carbon. If a body weighs 70kg, it holds about 16kg of carbon that comes from carbon dioxide photosynthesised by the vegetables eaten.

This carbon went through soil countless times since the beginning of the Earth. The calcium, sodium, potassium, and phosphorus inside our bodies all came from the vegetables that took up these elements from the soils. Even if one is mostly carnivorous, the animals consumed took those elements from the vegetables they grazed on.

In Genesis, however, dirt is also God's creation that looked good to God. It is the clay-built proto-human that receives God's breath. It is precisely because the soils are a receiver that soils are a giver: we came from it and go back to it. We share this fate with other living things.

Soil is the melting pot of all living things — including our own species — on the land.

Kyungsoo Yoo
is a soil scientist and professor
at the University of Minnesota, USA

Changing Hearts and Minds Organically

"If we do not permit the Earth to produce beauty and joy, it will in the end not produce food, either"

– Joseph Wood Krutch, American environmentalist (1893–1970)

There are many reasons why I decided to begin farming organically. I grew up on the farm I now care for, and had seen the wildlife diminish as our farming system changed and the hedges were demolished to make way for bigger machines. We were producing commodities that were guaranteed a market regardless of whether customers liked or needed what we produced; and I could not believe that the subsidies and market support we were receiving could possibly continue for much longer. We needed to connect with society's changing aspirations for food, become more 'market focused.'

And while doing my degree in agricultural technology, I had visited intensive pig and poultry enterprises for the first time. I was

There is not an animal that lives on the Earth, nor a bird that flies on its wings, but forms part of communities like you.

– Qur'an 6:38

appalled by the conditions that animals were living in, and determined to show that it could be done differently. I was interested in health, too, though not initially convinced that organic approaches were important in this regard. But as we started to experiment with the system, I could see the benefits. Simple but vital changes, like the requirement to feed ruminants mainly on forages like grass and clover rather than concentrated feeds such as grains and soya, stopped many health problems in our dairy cows.

Our free range organic pigs hardly ever need antibiotics, as their early introduction to soil, fresh air and green feed, plus later weaning from their mothers, keep them in fine fettle. Even my sceptical father agreed that he had never seen our animals looking so well. I had concerns about the health and welfare of our staff too. Farm workers were poorly paid and housed, and working in difficult, often dangerous conditions. Farms everywhere were cutting labour as they specialised and mechanised. Farms our size might only be employing one or two staff, so that any sense of community was destroyed, and people would often work long hours in isolation.

Photo courtesy of Helen Browning

Photo credit: Kevin van Bree

Keeping a mixed, vibrant farm allowed us to keep a big team, which has maintained the feel of the village as a working place, not a pretty dormitory for Swindon — the nearby big town — and has also helped to keep the school (and the pub, which we now run too!) viable.

it's not what you do but the way you do it, and why

I was not convinced that organic farming was the way forward when I started, but it seemed a vital experiment, to really test the system, and see how much great food we could produce while enhancing our environment, and respecting the animals and people who live on our farm. I have likened it to an athlete who decides to compete clean, to push the boundaries of his/her own abilities, without artificial aids. The past 27 years have been fascinating. Our original aims have been met in many ways, although the realities of working in an imperfect world mean that our business and farming system has often fallen short of our ambitions. We have needed to trade off between jostling priorities in a way that

is quite tough for us idealists, but has left me with at least some understanding of the challenges that businesses and governments face. The biggest learning of all, though, has been that all depends on attitude, spirit, motivation, values, and effort. There is no perfect system or way of doing anything.

Often, it's not what you do, but the way that you do it, and why. So the hardest bits of going over to an organic system on our farm have been all about changing hearts and minds, much more than the practical challenges. I reckon that applies in most spheres; that it is the organic principles of care, health, fairness, ecology that need to permeate all our decision-making, and that if they did, we would make more compassionate choices that would engage people in their implementation.

The Soil Association was founded to explore these issues, and to help our understanding of the interconnectedness of soil, plant, animal and humankind. This mission has energised me for many years, given that I have always been bemused by the ego of humankind!

We seem to feel that we can bend the world entirely to our will without regard for the rest of Nature. The tiny timescales in which our tiny, self-centred concerns and desires operate give little scope for the rational action that a bigger perspective demands, even a purely human-centric perspective.

As a farmer, I know that I will disrupt the natural world to produce food, fuel and fibre for people, and I want to tread as lightly as I can in doing this. I want to mimic and learn from the ecology of natural systems, to leave plenty of room for other species. I want a healthy, fair future for people; farming organically, and working with the Soil Association is my way of contributing to this possibility.

Helen Browning is Chief Executive of the Soil Association, which campaigns for planet-friendly organic food and farming.

Her organic farm is based in Wiltshire, Britain.

did you know?

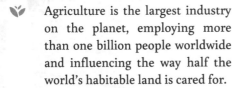 Agriculture is the largest industry on the planet, employing more than one billion people worldwide and influencing the way half the world's habitable land is cared for.

— World Wildlife Fund and United Nations Environment Programme

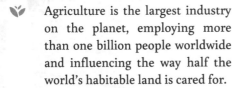 One third of all cereal crops and more than 90% of soya goes into animal feed, not food for humans.

— Compassion in World Farming

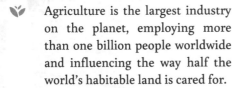 If all cereal were fed to people instead of animals, we could feed an extra 3.5 billion people.

— Soil Association

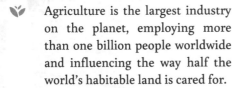 Women farmers produce more than half of all food worldwide.

— Food and Agriculture Organization

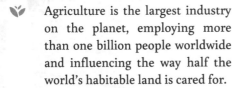 Britain has lost 97% of its fruit and vegetable varieties since 1900. Globally, 75% of the genetic diversity of crop plants was lost in the last century.

— Sustain

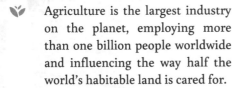 Every year, consumers in rich countries waste almost as much food (222 million tonnes) as the entire net food production of sub-Saharan Africa (230 million tonnes).

— United Nations Environment Programme

Business as Usual is not an Option

"Eating is an agricultural act"

— *Wendell Berry, American poet, philosopher and farmer*

We are now confronting one of the greatest challenges humanity has ever faced — the need to produce sufficient high-quality food on a diminishing area of agricultural land to nourish a peak world population of around nine billion, while at the same time addressing a combination of other factors. These have been referred to as the 'perfect storm' — namely climate change, population growth, diminishing resources and growing food insecurity.

After nearly a century during which most of us in the so-called 'developed nations' have dined out on the Earth's accumulated store of natural capital, plundering its reserves of soil, water and fossil-fuel energy and behaving as if there were an infinite supply of these resources when in fact they are absolutely finite, the crunch has now come. Today, the food systems responsible for feeding the vast majority of people are increasingly industrialised and globalised. Widespread damage is being done to the Earth's ecosystems through the use of chemical pesticides and nitrogen-based fertilisers. Yields of conventionally produced food are falling and soil is being degraded ten times faster than Nature can restore it.

It is becoming widely recognised, especially among people in positions of leadership, including government scientists and heads of NGOs, that only a change of unprecedented scale can enable the rapid transition to the more secure and sustainable food systems that are so urgently needed.

However, most people are unaware that business as usual is not an option. Such is the level of disconnection between many ordinary citizens and the story behind their food that most people are largely ignorant of the scale of the threat and the urgency of the need for a major transition of our food systems.

This brings into focus a very practical question. What is needed to bring about this radical transformation of our food systems, away from the present industrial and unsustainable approach and towards an alternative model that will provide healthy food for future generations without violating or depleting the natural capital of the planet?

people do not live by bread alone

This is where I believe the engagement of faith communities could assume a critical level of importance, since it is clear that the ecological crisis also has its spiritual counterpart. Realising the potential to create food systems which are truly sustainable and

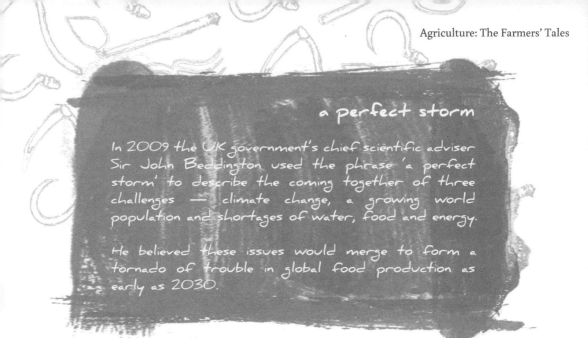

a perfect storm

In 2009 the UK government's chief scientific adviser Sir John Beddington used the phrase 'a perfect storm' to describe the coming together of three challenges — climate change, a growing world population and shortages of water, food and energy.

He believed these issues would merge to form a tornado of trouble in global food production as early as 2030.

resilient against external shocks will depend as much on inner conviction as it will on organised physical transformation, and if our actions are motivated only by self-interest and material gain, our work in the world will be certain to suffer accordingly, and in all likelihood fail to reach its potential.

It is in this sense that I believe the world's faith communities could play a central role in transforming our food systems. After all, they constitute more than two-thirds of the world's population, they think long term, they own significant amounts of the world's real estate, including farmland, and they have excellent communication networks.

In addition, and critically, they are also united by a sense of higher purpose, of stewardship, of respect for Nature and a recognition that unless both individual citizens and humanity as a whole can find our right places in attending to the physical whilst at the same time fulfilling our spiritual purpose, the change that is needed will simply not be possible.

Unless we bring a mindfulness that 'people do not live by bread alone' (Matthew 4:4), alongside all the structural changes that are required, to the way in which we produce, process, distribute and eat our food, it will simply not be possible to bring about change, either on the scale that is needed or in the time available. Conversely, I believe that if my outer efforts in the material world are nourished by a deep inner connection, only then will my work have the quality that is needed to support the emergence of landscapes that not only nourish their people but also serve a higher purpose.

Patrick Holden CBE is the founding director of the UK-based Sustainable Food Trust, a global voice for sustainable food systems.

Between 1995 and 2010, he was the Director of the Soil Association.

our dandelion summer

Patrick Holden has 40 years' experience of farming sustainably. His farm, Bwlchwernen Fawr, is the longest-established, registered organic dairy farm in Wales. As he wrote for the Sustainable Food Trust website, he has seen for himself how farming methods that avoid using chemical fertilisers and pesticides benefit wildlife while also producing our food.

Photo credit: Sustainable Food Trust

At certain times of the year many of our fields, especially those we have 'shut off' for hay or silage, acquire a golden yellow hue. This 'dandelion summer' lasts for a brief few days before the flowers turn into white clocks, releasing millions of tiny parachute seeds, after which the plants quietly recede into the vegetation of the sward, shaded out by more competitive clovers and rye grasses.

Many farmers think of dandelions as a weed, but I regard them as a wonderful gift of Nature, a free, nutritious and harmonious component of our long-term grassland pastures. In addition to looking so beautiful, their taproots draw up minerals from the subsoil, which is presumably why our dairy cows will selectively graze them at this time of year.

They are also a vital nectar source for bees — as I stood still to take photo-graphs, I became aware of a low back-ground buzzing and realised I was surrounded by bees working the flowers. It seemed to me that the scout bees from every hive for miles around had got the word out about the Bwlchwernen dandelion fields. The fact that our fields have all these dandelion and so many other wild plants that co-exist within a farming system primarily managed to feed dairy cows, is a direct consequence of our not having used any nitrogen fertiliser for 40 years.

What is Sustainable Agriculture?

Prince Charles has been talking about the future of food and farming for more than 30 years. As he told the Future for Food Conference at Georgetown University, Washington, DC, in 2011, 'I have all the scars to prove it! Questioning the conventional world view is a risky business.'

His understanding is rooted in his own experience of farming sustainably for nearly three decades. In his speech — which many described as groundbreaking — he set out what he meant by sustainable agriculture.

So what is a 'sustainable food production' system? We should be very clear about it, or else we will end up with the same system that we have now, but dipped in 'green wash'. For me, it has to be a form of agriculture that does not exceed the carrying capacity of its local ecosystem and which recognises that the soil is the planet's most vital renewable resource…

In my own view it is surely not dependent upon the use of chemical pesticides, fungicides and insecticides; nor, for that matter, upon artificial fertilisers and growth-promoters or GM [genetic modification]. You would have, perhaps, thought it unlikely to create vast monocultures and to treat animals like machines by using industrial rearing systems.

Nor would you expect it to drink the Earth dry, deplete the soil, clog streams with nutrient-rich run-off and create, out of sight and out of mind, enormous dead zones in the oceans. You would also think, wouldn't you, that it might not lead to the destruction of whole cultures or the removal of many of the remaining small farmers around the world? Nor, presumably, would it destroy biodiversity at the same time as cultural and social diversity.

On the contrary, genuinely sustainable farming maintains the resilience of the entire ecosystem by encouraging a rich level of biodiversity in the soil, in its water supply and in the wildlife — the birds, insects and bees that maintain the health of the whole system. Sustainable farming also recognises the importance to the soil of planting trees; of protecting and enhancing water-catchment systems; of mitigating, rather than adding to, climate change.

To do this it must be a mixed approach. One where animal waste is recycled and organic waste is composted to build the soil's fertility. One where antibiotics are only used on animals to treat illnesses, not deployed in prophylactic doses to prevent them; and where those animals are fed on grass-based regimes as Nature intended.

The speech on page 9 was reprinted with kind permission of HRH The Prince of Wales.

Read the speech in full on the Prince's website: **princeofwales.gov.uk**

Hymn to the Earth

Set me, Earth, amidst the nourishing strength
That emanates from the body.

The Earth is my mother, her child am I;
Infinite space is my father,

May he fill us with plenty.
Peaceful, sweet-smelling, gracious Earth.

Whatever I dig from thee, O Earth,
May that have quick growth again,

May we not injure your vitals or your hearts.

Full of sweetness are the plants
and full of sweetness
these my words.

– Atharva Veda, Book XII

Agriculture and Climate Change

Agriculture, including associated deforestation and changes in land use, is the second largest contributor of greenhouse gas emissions after fossil fuels, accounting for 25-30% of the total. But agriculture (including agroforestry) is also the only sector that can take carbon out of the atmosphere, says Rattan Lal, Professor of Soil Science and Director of Ohio State University's Carbon Management and Sequestration Center in the United States.

That means agriculture is the solution as well as the problem, he told the 2013 Borlaug Dialogue meeting in Iowa, US. 'The difference between fossil fuels and land use and soil is that with soil we can put back the carbon. If you take a three-metre depth, including the cryosoils — frozen soils — then the soils of the world contain about 4,000 gigatonnes of carbon.' This compares to about 600 gigatonnes stored in trees and all vegetation and about 800 gigatonnes in the atmosphere.

The problem is that most agricultural soils are seriously degraded, particularly in developing countries in Africa and South Asia. 'Because of past land use when we did not manage the land properly, because of soil erosion, because of extractive farming practice — taking away crop residues, not putting manure back — most soils in developing countries have lost 70-80% of their original organic carbon pool,' he said.

'There is a critical threshold level of organic matter content that soils should have to support life and crop growth. In most soils that level is 1.5-2%. Soils of Asia, West Africa and Punjab have 0.05%. As a result, these soils have lost their capacity to hold nutrients and fertilisers. 'So it is not just a matter of mitigating climate change. Our agricultural efficiency and productivity depends on [putting back] the organic matter content, which has been depleted. That is the way to increase food.'

Changing the way we farm can improve soil's capacity to hold water and encourage the vital biological activity undertaken by microorganisms and earthworms. 'Soil is like a bank account,' said Rattan. 'You can take out of it what you have put into it. If you take more out of it than you put into it, that's what leads to degradation and depletion.'

Leading environmental scientists predict that as many as 185 million Africans will die this century as the direct result of climate change...Climate change is real. It has begun.

– *Archbishop Emeritus Desmond Tutu, foreword to The Moral Ground*

six approaches to climate-smart agriculture

The United Nations Food and Agriculture Organization says we could drastically reduce carbon emissions from agriculture by changing the way we farm through:

- **Building soil fertility:** Reducing chemical use and tilling can rebuild dry or lifeless soils. Using the same land for crops and livestock can reduce overall carbon emissions.

- **Agroforestry:** Because trees remove carbon dioxide from the atmosphere, keeping them on farms can help mitigate climate change. Trees keep the soil healthier and more resilient, provide shade for livestock and create habitats for animals and insects that pollinate many crops.

- **Urban farming:** Growing food in cities means fewer greenhouse gas emissions because we don't have to transport so much food from rural to urban areas. It also means our cities have less concreted and paved land which reduces the risk of flooding.

- **Cover cropping:** Leaving soils bare in between crops contributes to soil erosion. Planting cover crops (also known as green manures) improves soil fertility and moisture by making soil less vulnerable to drought or heat waves. Mulching is another way to protect soils.

- **Water conservation:** Recycling wastewater in cities, using precise watering techniques such as drip irrigation rather than sprinklers, and catching and storing rainwater, all help reduce the strain on scarce water resources.

- **Preserving biodiversity and indigenous breeds:** We've lost a huge amount of crop diversity over the past century. Growing a wide range of locally adapted indigenous crops improves farmers' chances of withstanding the effects of climate change, such as heat stress, drought, diseases and pests.

FACT: In 1750, carbon dioxide in the atmosphere was at 277 parts per million. In 2012, it was at an average of 393 ppm, the highest for at least 800,000 years.

Photo credit: ARC

Putting Food on the Plate

Faith groups are some of the biggest deliverers of relief and development in Africa. The Evangelical Presbyterian Church of Ghana has been working in the country's hot, arid northern region for more than 50 years to support any community in need, both Christian and Muslim.

Once covered in thick forest, this region has been stripped of its trees by farmers and charcoal burners (almost everyone uses firewood for cooking), with the situation made worse by recurrent droughts and over-grazing by goats and cattle. Life is hard in this semi-desert — especially in the lean months in between harvests — and people are very poor. One of the Church's most successful initiatives in recent years is a dry-season gardening project, which has transformed the lives of people in a village in Yendi district, helping women feed their families at what is typically the leanest time of year.

Traditionally farmers plant their main crops, such as maize, during northern Ghana's rainy season and then live on the proceeds of the harvest for the remainder of the year. In a good year all is well, but in a bad year people go hungry. Charcoal-burning and firewood-harvesting supplement their income during the lean months but these activities only accelerate the environmental degradation that is a source of many of their problems.

The Evangelical Presbyterian Church of Ghana encouraged women to grow green leafy vegetables, tomatoes and peppers outside the traditional planting season for home use. The most immediate benefit was access to fresh vegetables. 'We plant and in three weeks, we can cut the leaves,' explained one woman. This ready supply of food had a big impact on people's health: 'You can see the freshness in our children's faces and also in the faces of the old people,' she added.

In fact, the project was so successful, the women grew so much they were able to sell their produce and earn much-needed income for their families. Soon the men were volunteering to water their wives' plots for them to ensure the vegetables were well cared for. This project succeeded because a ready source of water was available in the form of a dam built by Action Aid — another project in a different area failed for lack of water.

Great Idea!

You Can't
Cheat Nature

"The solutions to hunger and climate change begin at the end of your fork"

— Small Planet Institute

One billion people are without enough food; two billion people are cursed with diseases linked to bad food. And it is all related to the way food is being produced. It is an economic and public health disaster.

Industrial agriculture, sold as the 'Green Revolution' and the 'Second Green Revolution' to developing countries, is a chemical-intensive, capital-intensive, fossil fuel-intensive system. We are repeatedly told we will starve without poisons and chemical fertilisers. However, chemicals undermine food security by destroying the fertility of soil, killing the biodiversity of soil organisms which are the real builders of soil fertility, the pollinators such as bees and butterflies without which plant reproduction and food production is not possible, and friendly insects which control pests.

Hunger and malnutrition are manmade; hunger is a direct consequence of the current industrialised food-production system. Nutrition in food comes from the nutrients in the soil. Industrial agriculture, which depends on synthetic nitrogen, phosphorous and potassium-based fertilisers, leads to the depletion of vital micronutrients and trace elements such as magnesium, zinc, calcium and iron.

The 'chemicalisation' of agriculture and food is a recipe for 'de-nutrification' of our food.

Industrially produced food is nutritionally empty mass, loaded with chemicals and toxins — foods such as white rice, white bread and yellow hybrid corn. To get the same amount of nutrition people need to eat much more food. The increase in 'yields' of empty mass does not translate into more nutrition. In fact, it is leading to malnutrition.

ours is a hunger-creating system

The current system is a hunger-creating system because it costs more to produce the food than can ever be earned back. It must, by its very structure, push farmers into debt, and indebted farmers everywhere are pushed off the land, as their farms are foreclosed and appropriated. In poor countries, farmers trapped in debt by purchasing chemicals and non-renewable seeds, sell the food they grow to pay back the debt. This unbearable pressure leads thousands of farmers to take their lives every year in India alone.

Photo credit: Meena Kadri

ity to produce food by destroying climate stability. As I stated in my book *Soil Not Oil*: 'Forty per cent of greenhouse gas emissions come from a globalised industrialised food system.'

Recently I debated with someone who said we had to 'engineer' the planet because we have to cheat Nature in order to solve the climate crisis. I said: 'Isn't it high time you realised that you can't cheat Nature?'

We have to take seriously the crisis of climate change, but we have to respond to it with our full ethical consciousness. That's why for me ecological agriculture is a climate solution. The problems caused by globalised industrial food production can be solved by moving towards sustainable systems of food production that work with, not against it.

Wherever chemicals and commercial seeds have spread, farmers are in debt, and lose entitlement to their own produce. They become trapped in poverty and hunger. And so the cycle continues.

A second level at which industrial chemical agriculture creates hunger is by displacing and destroying the biodiversity which provides nutrition. Thus in India the Green Revolution, which started in the 1960s, displaced pulses, an important source of proteins, as well as oilseeds. It therefore reduced nutrition per acre; it did not increase it.

The current large-scale method of agriculture requires vast amounts of water — and actually hinders our capacity to produce food by destroying the land's capability to store water. And it is destroying our capac-

Biodiversity-based, ecological farming produces more food per unit acre and produces more incomes for rural families. It produces healthier food, it reduces water use, and both absorbs carbon dioxide out of the atmosphere and builds up much-needed carbon. So, it is both a mitigation and adaptation strategy for climate change.

Dr Vandana Shiva is an Indian environmental activist and scientist, and author of more than 20 books, including **Violence of Green Revolution**.

She is Director of the Research Foundation for Science Technology & Ecology and founder of Navdanya, a national movement to protect the diversity and integrity of living resources, especially native seed.

Farming that Brings
Hope to the Hungry

"Give us this day our daily bread"

– The Lord's Prayer

A group of men and women are gathered in a field in Kenya measuring distances using lengths of string. Following them are others digging small holes at very precise angles and applying specific amounts of fertiliser and seed. There's a lot of laughter and animated talk, but also focus and concentration.

These pastors and church leaders from the Anglican and Catholic Churches in Kenya are learning a form of agriculture called Farming God's Way, which is not only helping to restore degraded land and protect the environment, but also increasing crop yields — sometimes significantly, by three, five or even ten times. In the words of trainer Craig Sorley, pictured right, of Care of Creation Kenya, it is a way of farming that 'gives glory to God and hope to the hungry'.

Agriculture is the backbone of sub-Saharan Africa, providing the biggest source of employment, livelihoods and foreign exchange. Yet African agriculture is in crisis: soils are worn out and agricultural production is falling. Africa's fragile soils suffer from a combination of poor agricultural practices, degradation of natural resources, overgrazing and the pressure of growing populations. Other problems include lack of access to land, particularly for women farmers. Most people farm on plots of two hectares or smaller, and these smallholder farmers provide as much as 90% of agricultural production in some countries.

As populations increase, the soil is worked harder on ever decreasing plots. The International Fertilizer Development Center (IFDC) estimates that sub-Saharan Africa loses around eight million tonnes of soil nutrients per year, and that more than 95 million ha of land has been degraded to the point of greatly reduced productivity. No wonder farming is seen as a profession of last resort: no one wants to be a farmer in Africa.

God is the 'Master Farmer'

So how is Farming God's Way transforming farming in Africa? This faith-based approach to farming is based on the idea that God is the Master Farmer and calls upon us to be faithful stewards of the land. 'Farming God's Way puts God back where He belongs — into the very centre of how we view and practice agriculture. This is a holistic approach that ministers to farmers, addressing the spiritual and physical roots of the decline that is taking place,' says Craig.

Photo credit: ARC

'For Christians, the story of agriculture begins in Eden with the knowledge that God was the one who planted a magnificent and diverse garden. This story brings tremendous meaning and dignity to the realm of agriculture. As Christian gardeners we need to follow the example of the First Farmer and uphold the Garden of Eden as a model to be pursued. The beauty of a healthy, productive and well cared for agricultural landscape should be a testimony to the Christian faith.'

How does it work? In practice Farming God's Way is similar to conservation agriculture, which is promoted throughout the world by secular groups such as the UN's Food and Agriculture Organization as a form of climate-smart agriculture that both restores degraded land and increases crop yields. As well as reducing drudgery for smallholder farmers, this farming method nourishes the soil and enables it to retain water much better, which means it is particularly useful in dry areas.

The difference with Farming God's Way is the latter is based around Biblical teachings. 'Conservation agriculture is Farming God's Way without God. But it's the God part of this picture that really changes attitudes,' says Craig. He explains the core principles:

- **Minimal disturbance of the soil** (no tillage). Ploughing destroys soil structure including the microorganisms that live in the soil, leading to erosion and rapid water loss.

- **Permanent organic cover** in the form of mulch. 'In Creation we observe that God does not leave the soil bare.' This improves the soil's ability to absorb water and adds organic matter.

- **No burning of crop residues**, as is common in African agriculture. These are used to cover the soil instead.

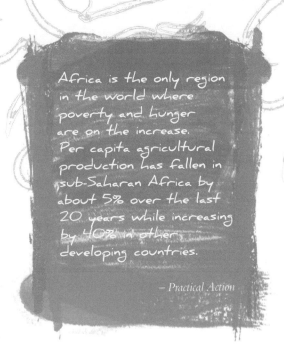

Africa is the only region in the world where poverty and hunger are on the increase. Per capita agricultural production has fallen in sub-Saharan Africa by about 5% over the last 20 years while increasing by 40% in other developing countries.

— *Practical Action*

🌱 **Crop rotation**, which reduces the build-up of crop-specific pest and disease problems.

our land will be richer

In Kijabe, west of Nairobi, Craig grows crops using Farming God's Way methods and conventional agriculture to compare how well they do. His plots are just a few years old; with every year, the soil will become richer and more productive.

Even so, he's already seen big differences. In 2012 he harvested 89kg of potatoes from his Farming God's Way plot and just 51kg of potatoes from the conventional plot. His bean harvest was even more impressive — three-and-a-half times as much from the Farming God's Way plot compared with the conventional plot.

'They are planted on the same day, same variety, same small amount of inorganic fertiliser applied and this is all rain-fed agriculture,' he says. 'The beauty of this is that it's simple, it's achievable, you use your own resources in the community — you don't have to bring in fertilisers and seeds from the outside. It's just a change in commitment to the soil itself. If we restore the soil we will bring more food into our families.'

His results are echoed elsewhere in Africa where similar techniques are applied. In Uganda, for example, the Ministry of Agriculture, Animal Industry and Fisheries reports crop yields up to 600% higher with farms using conservation agriculture.

Augustine Muema Musyimi of the Methodist Church in Kenya attended one of Craig's workshops and says: 'We've trained people to understand what the Lord says about farming and because we are Christians that really resonates with us. We feel that we need to take care of Creation and of the way we are farming.

'What do I think? That farming will be transformed across Kenya, that many people will learn to farm in a way that glorifies the Lord and our produce will increase. We will conserve our land and it will be richer.'

When ARC's Muslim faith partners heard about Farming God's Way at an ARC meeting in Nairobi, Kenya, in 2012, they asked ARC to develop a faith-based approach to agriculture for Muslim farmers. See page 138.

Food and Worship in Christianity

"We give you thanks, most gracious God, for the beauty of the earth and sky and sea;

for the richness of mountains, plains, and rivers;

for the songs of birds and the loveliness of flowers.

We praise you for these good gifts and pray that we may safeguard them for our posterity."

– The Book of Common Prayer, Episcopal Church, 1979

Living in 'Right Relationship' with our Creator

"The world is charged with the grandeur of God"

— God's Grandeur, *Gerald Manley Hopkins*

As Christians, we believe that the world is 'charged' with God's Spirit, that the Earth has been created in love and that God cares deeply for all He has made. To love God, therefore, also means to love the Earth. Just as it would make no sense to declare great love of an artist such as Rembrandt and then destroy his art, it is contradictory to proclaim to love God and yet destroy what He has made.

From a Christian point of view, today's widespread environmental degradation is a consequence of our broken relationships with God, one another and other creatures. Thus, the current environmental crisis is at root, a spiritual crisis. The redemption and restoration of the creation is intertwined with human repentance and a desire to live in 'right relationship' with our Creator and His creation. As St Paul wrote in his letter to the Romans, 'the creation waits in eager expectation for the sons of God to be revealed' (Rom. 8:19). So, the Christian Gospel is good news not just for humans, but for the whole Earth. Ultimately, our hope is in a living, loving God, incarnate in Christ Jesus, who graciously forgives our sins and brings healing and restoration to all things.

In the British city of Bristol, where my husband Will and I live, we seek to love God's creation as best we can, trying to cultivate sustainable habits that bless rather than degrade it. One particular aspect of sustainable living that really excites us is the area of food and farming, since eating is the most direct way in which many of us — especially urbanites — encounter creation on a daily basis.

The way we eat and the choices we make about our food are far-reaching and have enormous potential to either 'bless' or degrade creation. By eating well we can nurture the soil, encourage good animal welfare and foster thriving local economies. By eating ignorantly we facilitate the degradation of soil, increase demand for abusive 'factory farms' and advance the colonisation of our local economies by distant corporations.

we are on a journey

It seems that one of the fundamental reasons we currently have such an ecologically destructive food system is due to the severing of relationships at various levels in our food economy. Thus, one of the key ways in which Will and I seek to eat more sustainably is by actively making mental and material connections around our food in an attempt to foster a deep awareness and appreciation of the complex relationships involved in food production. We are very much 'on a journey' in this sustainable food adventure but have found adopting a few simple habits to be very helpful.

An important habit for us is saying grace at meal times — thanking the Creator for His provision and recognising the value and the gift of the food set before us. Correspondingly, we have found telling stories about the origin of the food on our plates to be immensely helpful, enabling us to recognise the diverse people and places that have nurtured the produce we are eating.

Another crucial way of connecting with local producers and fostering more holistic relationships around food has been through farm visits. By getting to know the people and places that produce our food we are also now much more aware of the challenges and needs of our local farmers. A slightly more hard-line habit we have undertaken is giving up supermarket shopping and buying only from local independent stores, though I should note that we are blessed by an abundant array of local shops in Bristol, and we do 'skip' supermarkets to salvage perfectly edible food that would otherwise be discarded in landfill sites.

For those unacquainted with the term 'skipping', it means late night, under-cover food rescue operations from supermarket bins. For us, 'skipping' is a form of civil disobedience confronting the sacrilege of food waste. It's not everyone's cup of tea, of course, but certainly one small way to curtail the excessive amount of food waste that occurs across our cities on a daily basis.

Lastly, growing some of our own food, foraging with friends, taking time to make jams and experimenting with cooking uncommon, frequently wasted foods has also been hugely valuable in building relationships and seeing food as a gift. For Will and me, a sustainable approach to food and farming affects every area of life. Ultimately, we try to live in a spirit of gratitude, interacting with creation in a way that honours the Creator. In line with this thinking, we have founded a small Christ-centred agrarian community called Cactus, which seeks to actively care for creation in our urban context.

the joy of skipping

Pip writes: 'Vast amounts of delicious food consistently get thrown away by supermarkets due to mismanaged orders, faulty fridges and freezers, damaged packaging or food reaching 'Best Before' dates. For example, in one month we had two different nights where we went skipping at our local supermarket and each time found seven or eight large bins, full to the brim, of ice cream. We phoned friends and also dropped large quantities off at a local vicarage and community house, but we could still only recover a tiny fraction of what we found, the rest will all have gone to waste.'

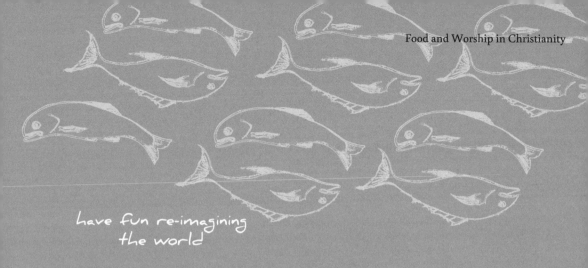

have fun re-imagining
the world

At the moment, we have Cactus Days on the first Saturday of each month, where a small group of us meet together at our home for a time of reflection, followed by some kind of action and then lastly, celebration. The reflections are either led by Will and I, drawing on poems, Biblical passages, articles and songs, or we invite others to share their stories; for example, at a recent Cactus Day we were blessed to have Chris Sunderland, director of the Bristol Pound, speaking about faith-informed local action. (The Bristol Pound is Britain's first city-wide currency; we try to use it wherever possible to support the local economy and Will is paid a percentage of his salary in Bristol Pounds.)

After our reflection stage, we then venture out to take part in some kind of agrarian activity, generally oriented around urban agriculture. We have adopted a few large raised beds in the 'Bear-pit' — a very large, sunken roundabout situated in central Bristol renowned as a homeless hangout — where we have planted an apple tree and are growing carrots, kale, parsnips, sunflowers, salads and lots of 'skipped' mint. After tending

our 'Bear-pit' beds, or getting involved in other urban farming activities, we then enter our time of celebration, where we generally share food together (foraged, grown, skipped, or bought!).

In the future, Will and I would love to have a Cactus house here in Bristol, where a group of us could live together demonstrating urban creation care and exploring new ways of sustainable living. Our dream would be to also have a Cactus Café, a not-for-profit initiative that serves the community and acts as a hub for urban food and sustainable farming initiatives, with workshops, talks, films and music. For now, though, our hope is to learn together, encourage one another to love creation more deeply, and have fun re-imagining the world.

As well as studying theology and environmental ethics, **Pip and Will Campbell-Clause** have pioneered urban food growing projects and worked on organic farms in Britain and USA.

The Meal at the Heart of Christian Practice

"For I was hungry and you fed me; I was thirsty and you gave me drink"

— Matthew 25:35

In many Christian traditions, celebration of the Eucharist or Lord's Supper is the heart of the practice of faith. In the eating of bread and the drinking of wine, the faithful receive Jesus Christ as food and nurture so they can be empowered to share God's love and nurture in the world. According to John's gospel — 'He who eats My flesh and drinks My blood abides in Me, and I in him' (John 6:56) — Christians 'eat' Jesus as the 'bread of life' so that he will abide in them, transform them from within, and thus enable them to share in God's healing, feeding, and communion-building ways with the world.

That a meal should be at the heart of Christian practice should not surprise us, particularly when we recall that food is one of God's most primordial ways of demonstrating love in the world. From the very beginning of scripture (Genesis 2), God is the primordial and essential Gardener breathing life into the soil that gives life and food to every creature.

Understood in a Christian manner, food is never simply a commodity or fuel subject to the economic logics of efficiency and profitability or the consumer logics of convenience and a cheap price. Food is God's love made sensual and delectable. It is a costly

love, because for any creature to eat, other creatures must die.

How does anyone become worthy of receiving another's life and death? The life and ministry of Jesus teaches that to become worthy we must offer our lives in service to others. Just as Jesus demonstrated an hospitable and celebratory way of being in the world — he was known as the glutton and drunkard who ate with sinners — so too followers of Jesus bear witness to God's love by showing hospitality to others, feeding them good food and extending the table of fellowship to all that are met. For good reason, some theologians refer to God's work of creating and sustaining the world as one lavish act of hospitality that 'makes room' for creatures to flourish and to be.

Jesus reveals the deep meaning of food as fellowship. Though we may at times eat alone, the truth of the matter is that every time we take a bite of food we are implicated in vast webs of relationships that join us to fellow eaters, cooks, gardens, agricultural fields, and uncountable animals, plants, and microorganisms. From a Christian point of view, the decisive question is whether or not our eating is 'good news' to the creatures we eat and live among. Early Christians believed that the gospel is not

> Every time we take a bite of food we are implicated in vast webs of relationships that join us to fellow eaters, cooks, gardens, agricultural fields, and uncountable animals, plants, and microorganisms.

restricted to people ('This is the gospel that you heard and that has been proclaimed to every creature under heaven', Colossians 1:23). They also believed that Jesus intends to reconcile all creatures in heaven and on Earth (Colossians 1:20).

Church-supported agriculture and church-sponsored community gardens are but two examples of ways this good news is being worked out today. Rather than simply accepting the industrial methods of food production that poison land and water, abuse animals, and degrade agricultural workers, a growing number of Christians and church communities are growing healthy, poison-free food in ways that honour God and respect fellow creatures. Rather than collecting and handing out highly processed and artificially flavoured foods to the poor and hungry in their communities, they are distributing fresh vegetables and fruit or inviting them in to meals cooked with healthy and whole ingredients.

Living in the midst of a food industry and culture that, in many ways, continues to be a desecration to God and violation of fellow creatures, Christians are learning that their faith calls them to be more merciful, responsible, and hospitable eaters in the world. Neither food nor life is cheap. Each is a costly gift that is only properly received when people, like Jesus Christ, turn their lives into gifts for the feeding and nurture of each other.

Norman Wirzba is Professor of Theology and Ecology at Duke Divinity School, Durham, North Carolina, USA.

His most recent book is **Making Peace with the Land**, co-written with Fred Bahnson.

He is also the author of **Food and Faith: A Theology of Eating**.

Christian Dietary Rules

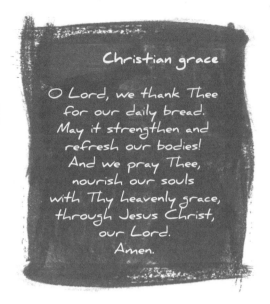

Christian grace

O Lord, we thank Thee
for our daily bread.
May it strengthen and
refresh our bodies!
And we pray Thee,
nourish our souls
with Thy heavenly grace,
through Jesus Christ,
our Lord.
Amen.

Christianity — in its many and varied forms — is the world's largest faith numerically, with more than 2.1 billion followers worldwide. While there are traditions of fasting (Lent and Advent) and monastic traditions of weekly fasts, there are no specific dietary rules. Indeed, in the New Testament, there is a story told in The Acts of the Apostles that deliberately breaks Christianity from the older Jewish prohibitions on certain foods. In Acts 10:9–30 Peter is on a roof top when he falls into a trance and sees a huge sheet coming down from Heaven with every kind of living creature upon it. A voice says: 'Now Peter, kill and eat.' To an Orthodox Jew this was horrendous but Peter interprets this to mean that there can be no barriers — religious or otherwise — between Jews and Gentiles.

The role of food as communal and as communion with God is found in the Eucharist or Mass, when bread and wine is shared in a re-enactment of the Last Supper, the final meal that Jesus Christ had with his disciples.

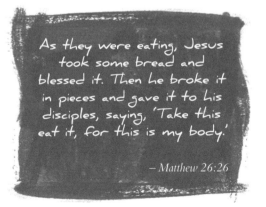

As they were eating, Jesus took some bread and blessed it. Then he broke it in pieces and gave it to his disciples, saying, 'Take this eat it, for this is my body.'

— *Matthew 26:26*

Catholics traditionally abstained from eating meat on Fridays in commemoration of the day Jesus Christ was crucified but they were allowed to eat fish. While this tradition declined from the 1970s onwards, it has recently been revived as part of Catholic ecological awareness about the environment and food.

Catholicism's Friday abstinence rule was the reason why McDonald's created its Filet-o-Fish sandwich, according to Michael Foley in *Why Do Catholics Eat Fish on Friday?* (Palgrave Macmillan), who says hamburger sales fell significantly on Fridays in a largely Catholic part of Cincinnati so the franchise owners introduced the fish sandwich and sales picked up again.

The monastic system of weekly fasting lies at the heart of the popular 5:2 fasting diet — two days of fasting and five days of normal eating every week. Studies of Greek Orthodox monks in the 1990s showed they were far less likely to suffer from heart attacks or strokes than men who were not in monastic orders or following the monastic fasting rules.

Christian Festival Food

Easter

Easter is the most sacred Christian festival of the year. Good Friday, which recalls the crucifixion and death of Jesus, is meant to be a day of fasting; Catholic adults, for example, are expected to avoid meat on that day. Easter Sunday is known as the joyous 'feast of feasts', when the faithful celebrate the fundamental truth of their faith — the resurrection of Jesus Christ.

Easter is preceded by Lent, a period of prayer, penance and abstinence based on Jesus Christ's 40 days of temptation in the wilderness (Luke 4:1–2). Many Christians will give up meat during this time, or abstain from a favourite food or activity as a self-discipline that recalls Jesus Christ's sacrifice and withdrawal into the desert for 40 days.

The following pages show two recipes used at this time.

Recipe...

Hot Cross Buns

Hot cross buns are eaten hot or toasted on Good Friday with the cross standing as a symbol of the Crucifixion. These spiced buns made with currants or raisins (special treats to celebrate the end of the fasting period of Lent) are believed by some to pre-date Christianity, although the first recorded use of the term 'hot cross bun' was not until 1733.

Ingredients

(Use planet friendly, fairly traded, free-range ingredients wherever possible.)

For the buns:

500g / 1lb 2oz / 3 and a third cups strong white bread flour

Half tsp salt

2 heaped tsp mixed spice

50g / 2oz caster sugar

50g / 2oz butter, chopped into cubes

200g / 7oz mixed dried fruits

7g sachet easy-blend dried yeast

200ml / 7fl oz / 3 quarters cup milk

2 eggs

For the crosses and glazes:

3 tbsp plain flour

2 tbsp water
(enough to make a paste)

Honey for glazing

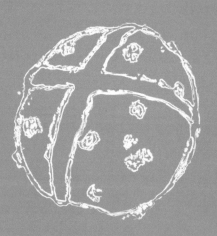

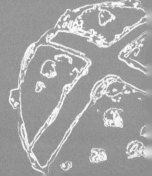

Method

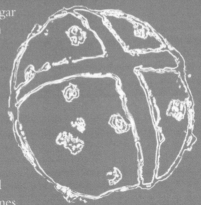

Put the flour, salt, mixed spice and sugar into a bowl and mix well. Rub in the butter with your fingertips, add the dried fruit, then sprinkle over the yeast and mix.

Slowly warm the milk until it is hot but cool enough to put your finger in for a couple of seconds. Beat the milk with the eggs. Gradually pour into the dried ingredients — don't add it all in one go in case the mixture becomes too wet. Add a little more milk if necessary.

Using a blunt knife, mix the ingredients to a moist dough, then leave for five minutes. Take out of the bowl and cut the dough into eight equal pieces. Shape into buns on a floured surface and space on a baking sheet.

Loosely cover with oiled cling film and leave in a warm place until it has expanded to half again in size. This will take anything between 45 minutes and 1 hour 15 minutes, depending on how warm the room is.

When the buns are risen, heat oven to 220C/fan 200C/gas 7. Mix 3 tbsp flour with 2 tbsp water to make a paste. Pour into a plastic food bag and make a nick in one of the corners so that you can pipe crosses on top of each bun.

Bake for 12–15 minutes until risen and golden. Trim any excess cross mixture from the buns and brush all over with honey.

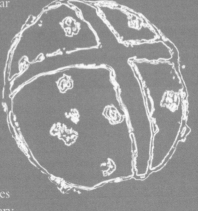

The buns will keep fresh for a day. After that they are best toasted and served with butter.

Tsoureki

In the Greek Orthodox Church, everyone gathers for the midnight Service of the Resurrection on Holy Saturday.

Afterwards, people go home to break their Lenten fast with a light lamb soup called 'mayiritsa', and a traditional Easter bread, tsoureki. This is a rich, brioche-like, often plaited bread flavoured with orange and a distinctive spice called 'mahlab' or 'mahlepi', which is made from the ground up pips of wild cherries and is also widely used in Middle Eastern cooking.

Some people bake tsoureki with hard-boiled eggs coloured red to symbolise Christ's blood.

Ingredients

(Use planet friendly, fairly traded, free-range ingredients wherever possible.)

Buy mahlepi from specialist Greek or Arabic food stores or order online. Mahlepi adds a nutty, slightly sour flavour so if you can't find it, you could replace it with ground Chinese almonds, or ground fennel seeds or cardamom.

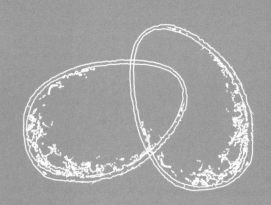

For the tsoureki:

500g / 1lb 2oz / 3 and a third cups plain flour

21g / 3 quarters oz dried yeast

125ml / 4fl oz / half cup milk

100ml / 3 and a half fl oz /half cup lukewarm water

2 eggs, lightly beaten, plus extra for brushing

50g / 2oz caster sugar

Finely grated rind of 2 oranges

2 tsp mahlepi spice

75g / 3oz softened butter, coarsely chopped, plus extra to serve

For the eggs:

3 eggs

Red food colouring

Method

Combine flour, yeast and a
pinch of salt in a bowl,
form a well in the centre.
Add milk, eggs, sugar,
orange rind, the mahlepi or
alternative spice, and the
lukewarm water and mix
until a soft dough forms
(five to seven minutes). If
you have an electric mixer
fitted with a dough hook, it
might be easier to use this than
kneading by hand.

Gradually add butter, a little at a
time, mixing until a smooth soft
dough forms (another three to five
minutes), place in a lightly greased
bowl, cover with cling film and set aside
until doubled in size. This will take
between 40 minutes and one hour.

Meanwhile, for red Easter eggs, follow
instructions on the packet of red food colouring
to cook and dye the eggs, then set aside to cool
completely.

Knock back the dough and divide into three pieces
if you want to create a plait. Roll each piece into a
45cm-long cylinder, plait pieces together, then bring
ends together to form a wreath and squeeze to join. Place
on an oven tray lined with baking paper and set aside to prove
slightly (20 minutes).

Preheat the oven to 180C/fan 160C/gas 4. Brush the wreath with a little
egg, wash and then gently push red Easter eggs (unpeeled) into the wreath
and bake until the wreath is golden and cooked through (25–30 minutes).

Cool on a wire rack and serve with butter.
Greek Easter bread is best eaten the day it's made.

And Wisdom Asks...

"So I decided there is nothing better than to enjoy food and drink and to find satisfaction in work"

— *Ecclesiastes 2:24*

'I am sorry to be so late, the traffic was terrible...' And Wisdom asks: 'The traffic? Don't you mean the cars ahead of you? You, the innocent victim. Those behind you non-existent.' Er, yes, maybe. I'm afraid most of my language is from my own point of view, my vested interests.

I go shopping. Am about to pick and choose as if food began its life on the shelves. And Wisdom asks: 'Weren't you going to use your LOAF and buy Locally produced, Organically grown, Animal-friendly, Fairly traded goods?' Er, yes, maybe. But it takes much more focus and care to do that. And what difference will little me make when all those with heaped-up trolleys don't care?

I buy a can of drink, interested in the drink, of course. And Wisdom whispers: 'What about that programme you heard on the radio about the dire conditions of miners in Latin American aluminium mines?

'And why, why are those at the beginning of tin can production on starvation wages when the director of the can company earns a fortune?' Er, yes, thanks. Can't do much about that. But I can live with the question and try to recycle more aluminium.

It's no wonder that Jesus urges us to take care of the way we see and hear things. He found, increasingly I think, that very gifted people (especially gifted with learning, wealth or social authority) often became so preoccupied with their own way of seeing or hearing that they could not stand back and see what was really going on.

Beware you who are wealthy, not because you are sinners but because you have created your own 'kingdom', your own self-justifying language and awareness.

One of his most striking parables is when the invitation goes out to enter the banquet of real life (Matthew 22:2–6) in which Jesus says, 'The Kingdom of Heaven can be illustrated by the story of a king who prepared a great wedding feast for his son. When the banquet was ready, he sent his servants to notify those who were invited. But they all refused to come.

'So he sent other servants to tell them, "The feast has been prepared. The bulls and fattened cattle have been killed, and everything is ready. Come to the banquet!" But the guests he had invited ignored them and went their own way, one to his farm, another to his business. Others seized his messengers and insulted them and killed them.'

If this were today, the first couple would be preoccupied by a newly bought house and so can't see further than that. The second

Photo credit: Kevin Rawlings

It is, in fact, in our social teaching down through the years that anything anyone has in excess of reasonable need belongs (in justice not largesse) to those in need. That truth is our best-kept secret.

there is a radical transformation of bread and wine

For many Christians the feeding of the 5,000 should be taken as the model for our Eucharist or Communion services. So we should keep an open table to anyone of goodwill who comes for Communion. In the Catholic faith, however, Communion at the Eucharist is more profound than that, and if we read John's sixth chapter it seems to have been a real issue in the early church.

Let me share some personal experiences as a Catholic priest. Each Sunday evening I celebrate the Eucharist with a hundred or so Catholics. I am deeply moved at the time of Communion by their 'Amens' to the words 'the Body of Christ, the Blood of Christ'.

On the day before he was crucified, at what is known as 'The Last Supper', Jesus was with his friends 'and he took bread, gave thanks and broke it, and gave it to them, saying, "This is my body given for you; do this in remembrance of me." In the same way, after the supper he took the cup, saying, "This cup is the new covenant in my blood, which is poured out for you."'

would have just bought a new car and would be keen to take it out for a drive. The gospel Jesus lived and urged us to make our own is a radical critique of the market economy as an ideology. Any idea that if we all look after our own, the common good will see to itself is a very plausible illusion. And, like all ideologies, carries within itself the seeds of its own downfall.

One possible reading of Jesus 'feeding the 5,000' (as recorded in John 6:5–13) is that he knew there was enough food in that vast gathering if only the families who had food could be persuaded to relinquish their hold on private property and learn to share. His initial act of blessing and sharing those few loaves was a trigger sacrament for all to do likewise. It would be wonderful indeed if our churches could teach and live like that.

I know that the 'Amen' of each communicant is deeply personal but is not private, because each of us receives [Holy Communion] as a member of the Church of which we are members in our wider lives. There is a radical transformation of bread and wine into becoming the Body and Blood of Christ, not because I believe it, not because I understand it, or anyone understands it, but because it is the faith — knowledge of the Church.

It has come home to me more and more through involvement with Oxfam, CAFOD (the official Catholic aid agency for England and Wales) and the Justice And Peace Network over the years, that the special moment of our 'Amen' in Communion sends us out to break bread in our economic and political lives during the week.

Would that all of us Catholics who say 'Amen' on a Sunday also said 'Amen' to our Church's true tradition.

Father Tom Cullinan is a monk-priest of the Archdiocese of Liverpool, Britain.

He is the author of books including **Eucharist and Politics, If the Eye be Sound** and **The Passion of Political Love.**

feeding the five thousand

Jesus soon saw a huge crowd of people coming to look for him.

Turning to Philip, he asked, 'Where can we buy bread to feed all these people?' He was testing Philip, for he already knew what he was going to do. Philip replied, 'Even if we worked for months, we wouldn't have enough money to feed them!'

Then Andrew, Simon Peter's brother, spoke up. 'There's a young boy here with five barley loaves and two fish. But what good is that with this huge crowd?'

'Tell everyone to sit down,' Jesus said. So they all sat down on the grassy slopes. (The men alone numbered about 5,000.) Then Jesus took the loaves, gave thanks to God, and distributed them to the people. Afterward he did the same with the fish. And they all ate as much as they wanted.

After everyone was full, Jesus told his disciples, 'Now gather the leftovers, so that nothing is wasted.' So they picked up the pieces and filled 12 baskets with scraps left by the people who had eaten from the five barley loaves.

– John 6:5–13

what is LOAF?

*L*OAF *was developed by the UK group Christian Ecology Link to encourage Christians to buy food more ethically. LOAF is full of symbolic meaning for Christians, with Jesus describing himself as 'the bread of life'.*

The acronym comes from:

Locally Produced: Buying food from local and regional sources means fewer climate-damaging food miles, less lorry traffic, fewer new roads and runways, support for the local economy and local farmers and regional variety.

Organically Grown: Organic food is good for the environment and may be better for our health. We have a duty to take care of the Earth — 'The Lord God placed the man in the Garden of Eden to tend and watch over it.' (Genesis 2:15).

Animal Friendly: Our fellow creatures, including farm animals, are sensate beings. They feel pain and suffer when ill-treated. We have responsibilities from God to care for their welfare and to avoid abusing them.

Fairly Traded: Trade needs to be both sustainable and fair. Buying fairly traded foods means that workers who produce the food get a fair wage and better working conditions.

Christian Ecology Link asks churches to follow one or more of these principles when planning any communal meal.

LOFTY eating

During a rally on Making Poverty History in Edinburgh in 2005, one woman stood up and suggested LOAF should really be LOFTY — Local, Organic, Free-range, Traded Fairly and Yummy!

Use Your LOAF!

LOAF stands for food which is: Locally produced, Organically grown, Animal friendly and Fairly traded.

Thinking about Eating Ethically

"Never doubt that a small group of thoughtful, committed individuals can change the world, indeed it's the only thing that ever has"

— Margaret Mead, American cultural anthropologist

An old joke about us Presbyterians says that if we had been in charge of organising the Last Supper, it inevitably would have been called the Last Potluck Supper. Catholics, in my experience, match Protestants' love of eating meals together. But the reality is that neither group in the USA does very well when it comes to thinking about eating ethically.

Patrick Carter, a Catholic who graduated from Creighton University in Omaha, hopes to change that. He recently completed an independent research project there in which he sought to apply Catholic social teaching to producing and, especially, consuming food.

'We should first change ourselves,' Patrick told me. 'Buy local food, eat out less, eat less meat and don't overeat. We, as Christians, have a responsibility to care for God's creations — humans, animals, earth and water — and the way we currently grow and eat food is not reflective of this call. We can have a sustainable existence by first changing ourselves by buying locally grown and ethically harvested food that has a minimised impact on the environment.'

In other words, apply even to the dinner table the values drawn from Catholic social teaching. It's hard to imagine a place more suitable for teaching such values. As Patrick says, 'There is a tremendous amount of fellowship that exists at gatherings centred on food, faith and community. However, if the food would more closely reflect our Christian values to love the poor and care for God's creation, then the eaters could be in solidarity with the growers, the land, the farmers, the livestock, the harvesters and the hungry of the world in addition to the others in the room.'

I asked him if he thought there were Eucharistic implications for what he's advocating, and, sure enough, he said yes. 'Imagine,' he said, 'what a powerful statement of faith it would be if Christian communities purchased bread that was composed of ethically harvested and sustainably grown wheat. In our consumption of Christ we would accurately reflect our Christian faith to have a preferential option for the poor and to care for creation.'

> *Imagine what a powerful statement of faith it would be if Christian communities purchased bread that was composed of ethically harvested and sustainably grown wheat*
>
> *– Patrick Carter*

I'm regularly appalled by ways in which Americans view and treat food. Perhaps this comes from my childhood. My parents not only told me to clean my plate because children are starving in India but they actually moved our family to India for two years — not exactly to prove they were right but so my father could be part of a University of Illinois agriculture team that could help make Indian food self-sufficient.

So when I go to watch the Kansas City Royals play and, between innings, see the team mascot firing hot dogs at fans out of a giant air rifle, I often turn to the person next to me and sigh, 'Only in America.' And when I see the enormous food portions that restaurants regularly dish out, the plague of obesity in our country doesn't shock me.

Patrick thinks applying Catholic social teaching to food consumption would help with this problem, too: 'Diets composed of excessive meat, fat, sugar and calories —

along with a lack of fruits and vegetables have led,' he said, 'to a nation that has expanding waistlines and an increasing number of heart attacks, strokes and cancers.' Beyond that, he added, over-consumption and the manner in which we grow the food have 'harmful effects across the globe. For example, Americans' desire for beef results in huge areas of forest being cut down in Brazil in order to make space to grow cattle'.

Patrick is not the first person to think about the connection between food and ethical values, of course. He said, for instance, that he was influenced by some work in this field by John Sniegocki of Xavier University. I just hope he's not the last such person but is, rather, an early voice for important changes Americans should make.

Bill Tammeus, a Presbyterian elder and former award-winning Faith columnist for **The Kansas City Star**, writes a 'Faith Matters' blog (**billtammeus.typepad.com**).

This article first appeared in **National Catholic Reporter**.

on an altar surrounded with flies...

'I did not know how to keep the horseflies away from the chalice when I celebrated Mass that very same day with the scavengers in their tiny chapel. I did not know what to do with those that got into the wine in the chalice.

While I celebrated God's bounty in the Eucharist, I was surrounded by starving children with swollen bellies, many with pus-encrusted eyes, skin covered with boils. I winced every time they took my hand and touched it to their foreheads in reverence.

In my desolation, I raised the host as far as I was able, in my mind raising it higher than the summit of the garbage mountain, beyond the clouds and the stars, beyond the farthest quasar and supernova in the observable universe. 'On an altar surrounded with flies, accept, O Lord, this sacrifice.'

– *From* Faith and Hope on Smokey Mountain, *by Benigno Beltran*

What Kind of Person do We Want to Be?

Catholic priest Father Benigno Beltran, who works with slum dwellers in Manila, in the Philippines, issues this challenge to those of us promoting sustainability. It's not enough to talk about the need to protect the environment, he says; we are still not doing enough. Instead we need to ask a much deeper question: What kind of person do we want to be? By asking this question, we change people's mindset and motivate them to do something positive for the environment right now.

Fr Benigno spent 30 years as parish priest on a noxious rubbish heap called Smokey Mountain. Towering 20 storeys in height, it is home to a community of 25,000 people who scavenge the dump site for anything they can sell for food. In his book, *Faith and Hope on Smokey Mountain*, Fr Benigno tells the story of their struggle for hope and dignity amid the degradation and squalor of poverty — and how, through their eyes, he learned to read the Gospel anew.

Now as head of Veritas Social Empowerment Inc, which works to combat poverty in the Philippines, and inspired by his three decades among slum dwellers, he has begun a Care for the Earth project with Sacred Heart of Jesus Parish in another part of the Philippines, Quezon City, and the country's Philippines' Department of Agriculture to make sustainably grown food available to local people.

Farmers and fisherman from nearby provinces bring their naturally grown agricultural products to the Food Terminal Station in Sacred Heart Parish. These are sold to the member-families in strategic areas of the Basic Ecclesial Communities and a special ministry in the parish provides organic food to special children and cancer patients.

The project is co-ordinated by the parish and the hope is to show how sustainable community-based enterprises can network with other businesses in other localities and regions to improve their economic performance and provide sustainable food to local people.

Agriculture's 'hotspots' are red meat and dairy because they take more energy to produce and result in higher emissions of methane and nitrous oxide — greenhouse gases that are respectively 23 and 296 times more potent than carbon dioxide, according to the Worldwatch Institute.

Call to Action: Eating

- Eat mindfully — we have three meals a day if we are lucky. Why waste one?

- Eat real food — minimally processed and produced in the most natural way. If in doubt, ask yourself if your grandmother would recognise it.

- Eat more vegetables, fruit and grains — it's better for you and the planet.

- Eat food that has been produced sustainably — that is, in ways that protect natural resources and enhance the health of both plants and animals.

- Avoid intensively farmed eggs, poultry and livestock. Instead, choose meat, dairy and eggs 'with a better story', that is organic, free-range or sustainably produced.

- Reduce your intake of meat — especially red meat — and dairy to lower your dietary carbon emissions. Why not make one day a week meat-free? Or commit to eating grass-fed meat only (as opposed to intensively reared animals fed largely on grains and other crops)?

- Cook more from scratch and use lids on pots — it saves 6% of the energy.

- Avoid eating from polystyrene or plastic.

- Around one third of all food gets lost or wasted worldwide. Don't waste food — serve smaller portions, followed by 'seconds' if desired, and use leftovers in another meal.

- The Japanese have a phrase — *hara hachi bu:* eat until you are eight parts (80%) full. So eat slowly. Stop before you're sated. It's not just about health, it's about eating your fair share of the world's resources.

Small changes can make big differences.

Commit to adopting one of these ideas in your daily diet.

Case Study

Organic, locally sourced meat and seasonal vegetables are on the menu at the atmospheric coffee house and café at The University Church of St Mary the Virgin, Oxford, Britain. The Vaults and Garden Café, formerly Oxford University's old congregation house which dates back to 1320, prides itself on offering food that is responsibly sourced, fairly traded and good value.

For example, the milk comes from a nearby dairy that has 17 Ayrshire milking cows fed on a mainly grass-based diet. The chickens are from a farm where they roam free, foraging and grazing from first light to dusk.

Seasonal produce is bought locally throughout the year.

Food and Worship in Hinduism

"May the Lord accept this, our offering, and bless our food that it may bring us strength in our body, vigour in our mind, and selfless devotion in our hearts for His service."

*– Swami Paramananda,
a Hindu food blessing*

Annadana: The Gift of Food

"When one's food is pure, one's being becomes pure"

– Chandogya Upanishad 7.26.2

The food we eat, the food that nourishes us is a gift from the Earth, from the sun, from millions of years of evolution. It is also a gift from the farmers, livestock herders, fisher folk who till the land, care for animals and harvest fish. When we forget the Earth from where we receive our food, food becomes non-sustainable. Food is life. Food is not just our vital need: it is the web of life.

As the Taittiriya Upanishad says:

'From food (anna), verily, creatures are produced

'Whatsoever (creatures) dwell on the earth...

'For truly, food is the chief of beings...

'Beings here are born from food, when born they live by food,

'On deceasing they enter into food.'

Food is alive: it is not just pieces of carbohydrate, protein and nutrient, it is a being, it is a sacred being, as the Taittiriyaka Upanishad makes clear: 'Verily, they obtain all food who worship Brahma as food.' In the words of Maha Ashwamedhika, 'The giver of the food is the giver of life, and indeed of everything else'. Therefore, anyone who desires wellbeing in this world and beyond should especially endeavour to give food.

Because food is the very basis of creation, food is creation, and it is the Creator. It is Divinity in the context of the way we live: there are all kinds of duties that we should be performing with respect to it. If people have food, it is because society has not forgotten those duties. If people are going hungry, society has moved away from the ethical duties related to food.

Annadana is the gift and giving of food. All other ethical arrangements in society get looked after if everyone is engaging in annadana on a daily basis. According to an ancient Indian saying: 'There is no dana [act of giving or generosity] greater than annadana and tirthadana — the giving of food to the hungry and water to the thirsty.'

That is why in the poorest of Indian huts you find the little earthen stove being worshipped; the first piece of bread is given to the cow, then you are required to find out who else is hungry in your area. Our being alive is based on the lives of all kinds of beings that have gone before us — our parents, the soil, the earthworm — and that is why the giving of food in Indian thought has been treated as everyday sacrifice that we have to perform.

Again, in the words of the Taittiriya Brahmana:

'Do not send away anyone who comes to your door without offering food and hospitality.

'This is the inviolable discipline of humankind: therefore have a great abundance of food and exert all your efforts towards ensuring such abundance, and announce to the world that his abundance of food is ready to be partaken by all.'

Thus from the culture of giving you have the conditions of abundance, and the sharing by all. In another scripture it is said:

'I forsake the one that eats without giving,

'I am the annadevtaa (the god of food, the divine in food);

'I come and go according to my own discipline,

'I nurture the one for whom giving carries the same significance as eating,

'To this one I reach in plenty: I remain out of reach of the other who eats without giving,

'Who amongst men can deter me, the annadevtaa, from my course?'

Photo credit: Astrid Schulz

When we forget our annadatas, the food producers, we create hunger and poverty. An agriculture without people becomes an agriculture dominated by agribusiness, by fossil fuels, by agrichemicals and poisons. There is a predominant myth that industrial corporate agriculture produces more food. This is what justifies destruction of small farms and small farmers.

However, this false productivity only measures commodities per labour input, not food and nutrition per unit of land or water or energy. On the one hand this hides the high output of small, biodiverse, organic farms. On the other hand it hides the high external input of industrial monocultures that use ten times more energy than they produce as food. Industrial farms also use ten times more water than ecological farms.

As a result, nutrition disappears from our farms along with the farmers. And the environment is burdened with toxics and greenhouse gases. Climate change, erosion of biodiversity, depletion and pollution of water are the consequence. If these costs were internalised we could not afford to eat poisoned foods.

Dr Vandana Shiva

It is the duty of a householder to feed first of all the children, the old members of the family, the brahmanas and the invalids. Besides that, an ideal householder is required to call for any unknown hungry man to come and dine before he himself goes to take his meals. He is required to call for such a hungry man thrice on the road. The neglect of this prescribed duty of a householder, especially in the matter of the old men and children, is unpardonable.

– *AC Bhaktivedanta Swami Prabhupada*

Food for Life through Loving Service

"Food and the eater: that is the extent of the whole world"

– Brihadaranyaka Upanishad, 1.4.6

Every day at five o'clock in the afternoon hundreds of women, girls and small children sit quietly in rows inside a school compound in the holy city of Vrindavan in northern India, with plates made of leaves on the ground before them. They are waiting to be served kitcheri, a stew of rice, lentils, beans and vegetables, and for many this might be their only meal that day.

'You don't have to look closely to notice that these guests are the poorest of the poor, shoeless, wearing mismatched, ill-fitting, torn and tattered clothes, with dust on faces and hair that has turned blond as a result of chronic malnutrition,' says Rupa Raghunath Das, founder of Food for Life Vrindavan, which provides these free meals.

As its name suggests, feeding people is a big part of what Food for Life Vrindavan does. In the two decades since it was founded, it has distributed more than 3.5 million meals to children, girls and women. It focuses on women and children in particular because it says they bear the brunt of poverty in India. Food for Life Vrindavan grew out of Rupa's experiences at an International Society for Krishna Consciousness temple distributing free food to the poor in Vrindavan. The city is in Uttar Pradesh, one of India's most impoverished states, and Rupa was inspired to start his own charitable organisation, beginning by providing food to pilgrims, widows, children and anyone else who needed it.

Food for Life Vrindavan started its first school after it realised that about 800 children were coming to eat at its free food distribution. 'Hardly any of them were going to school. So we thought, "Why not start some classes?" That is how it began and in the summer of 2000, we had our first evening classes,' says Rupa. Today around 1,500 nursery and older children attend classes every weekday, receiving free breakfasts and lunches alongside a free education.

But that's not all. The food distribution programme is just one of the many ways in which Food For Life Vrindavan helps the poorest and most vulnerable members of the community in the city and surrounding villages. As well as providing adult literacy classes, health education, social services and environmental initiatives such as tree planting and paper recycling, it also cares for cows in its goshala (protective shelter).

It has an organic farm and nursery where it grows vegetables such as broccoli, Swiss chard, asparagus, lettuce, cauliflower, cabbage and spinach for the local community, and its own kitchens. Rupa says: 'Thanks to the ample supply of cow dung available from our Care for Cows, we do not use any pesticide or fertilisers. We have been using a mixture of cow urine and neem leaves [bitter leaves from an indigenous Indian sacred tree] to protect small plants from bugs and insects. Now we will also be using aloe vera to protect plants' growth.'

The farm grows 265 fruit trees, including pomegranate, mango, guava, orange, lime and lemon. Rupa says: 'We take thousands of saplings to places which are destitute, desert-like and poor, such as the villages in and around the holy land of Vrindavan. By giving these trees we feed many, many generations to come as well.'

loving service

But perhaps the greatest gift that Food for Life offers is inspiration — inspiration to break the cycle of poverty and bring about positive change in the world. Rupa explains: 'In India, there are still millions of children from poor families who grow up without getting an education. At Food for Life Vrindavan's schools, we work to break the cycle of poverty, not only by giving children an academic education but also by inspiring them and teaching them that they can be agents of change.

'For example, at our schools, we work to create a culture of everyone pitching in to help out and willingness to helping others is fostered and rewarded. We are assisted in our efforts to create an atmosphere of service to each other by the Hindu practice of

bhakti, which is translated into English as 'loving service'.

'Bhakti is a spiritual activity and when Hindus offer flowers, water or incense to a statue or picture of God, it takes them beyond the material realm into the spiritual world. As God is not a material being, service to him is not an activity of the material world — so an act as simple as offering a flower to God takes one out of the material realm and into the spiritual realm.'

The principle of bhakti or loving service is practiced in Food for Life Vrindavan schools from the start of the day when the children take flowers and present them to their classmates and teachers at morning assembly. 'After one person has smelt the flower, the child takes the flower and presents it to the next person for them to smell also,' says Rupa.

'The feeling of having a supportive and loving community, of being able to co-operate with others and get their co-operation is what empowers religious communities to work together to make positive changes in the world. And the practice of contenting ourselves with simple, homely and God-given pleasures can enable us to rein in our destruction of the planet.'

Rupa Raghunath Das was given a Human Achievers Award in 2012 for his work empowering women and children by the Human Achievers Foundation, which recognises individuals 'whose lives exemplify the ideal of living for the sake of others'.

Hindu Dietary Rules

"From Earth herbs, from herbs food, from food seed, from seed human beings. Human beings thus consist of the essence of food"

– Taittiriya Upanishad

Hinduism is one of the world's largest religions with more than 950 million adherents. Almost all live in South Asia, mostly in India where more than 80% of people are Hindus. Hindus believe all living beings are sacred because they are manifestations of God, and should be treated with respect and compassion. This is because the soul can be reincarnated into any form of life. Because of this belief in the sanctity of life, many Hindus are vegetarian. As the Yajur Veda says: 'You must not use your God-given body for killing God's creatures, whether they are human, animal or whatever'.

Even if Hindus eat meat, almost all will avoid beef. The cow is revered in Hinduism and the five products of the cow — milk, curd, ghee, urine and dung — are used in *puja* (worship).

Hindus believe that what we eat determines our mental as well as physical state. Eating *sattvic* (pure) food helps us to become sattvic ourselves. If we eat animal and intoxicating foods, we may develop animal qualities; killing animals for food is also regarded as bad karma with negative consequences for everyone involved, including those eating the food.

For these reasons, devout Hindus avoid meat, fish, poultry, eggs, alcohol, caffeine and very spicy or sour foods. Strict practitioners also refrain from onion, garlic, mushrooms and leeks, foods which are believed to increase passion and ignorance.

Food is seen as a gift from God and plays an important role in Hindu worship. According to the Vedic scriptures, all food should be offered as a sacrifice to God before it is eaten. Fasting is seen as a way of purifying the body and mind, and enhancing concentration during meditation and worship.

Hindu food blessing

This ritual is one.
The food is one.
We who offer
the food are one.
The fire of hunger
is also one.
All action is one.

We who understand
this are one.

Hindu Festival Food

Aloo Posto

Dussehra: The Hindu calendar has at least 18 feast days including Dussehra, which falls in October or November. It commemorates the killing of the ten-headed demon Ravana by Lord Rama and the killing of demon Mahishasur by the goddess Durga. Aloo Posto, with the poppy seeds and red chillies giving it distinctive colour, is a dry accompaniment to rice and curry dishes.

Ingredients

(Use planet friendly, fairly traded, free-range ingredients wherever possible.)

For the buns:

3 or 4 potatoes, chopped

3 tbsp poppy seeds

3 green chillies

1 tsp cumin seeds

1 tsp turmeric powder

3 dried red chillies

Salt to taste

Fresh coriander for garnishing

Oil

Method

Roast the poppy seeds for about a minute. Grind the roasted poppy seeds and green chillies into a paste with some water.

Deep-fry the potatoes until they turn golden brown. Set aside.

In another pan, heat 1.5 tbsp of oil. Add the cumin seeds, turmeric powder and dried red chillies. Stir well until they begin to crackle. Add the poppy seed paste and salt. Cook for two minutes.

Add the potatoes and a dash of water and leave to simmer for seven to eight minutes.

Garnish and serve.

Burfi

Diwali: India's best-known Hindu festival is Diwali — 'Festival of Lights' — held at the end of October or beginning of November, and is one of the major celebrations in Hindu communities. It's an exuberant time of feasting. Earthenware oil or ghee lamps called diyas are lit in houses, shops and public places to drive away darkness, and lavish spreads of sweets and treats served up to friends and family.

Burfi sweets are one of the traditional favourites. This recipe comes from Bhaktivedanta Manor in Hertfordshire, Britain. In keeping with Bhaktivedanta Manor's principles about caring for cows, the milk powder in this recipe should be organic.

Ingredients

(Use planet friendly, fairly traded, free-range ingredients wherever possible.)

This recipe makes a large number of sweets to share.

1kg / 2.2lb / 8 cups organic milk powder

1kg / 2.2lb / 8 and three quarter sticks butter

1kg / 2.2lb / 5 cups sugar

1 litre / 1 and three quarter pints / 2 pints 3 fl oz full fat milk

500ml / 17 fl oz / 1 pint double cream

1 tbsp vanilla essence

Method

Melt butter in a heavy-based, wide pot, mix sugar, essence and half the milk, slowly add milk powder and alternate with milk and then cream. This is to avoid any lumps forming. Stir the soft mixture over a medium heat. As it gets closer to the cooking time it will splutter, so be careful. Try using a long spoon.

The mix is ready when it leaves the side of the pot clear. Take out a small ball the size of a peanut and leave it to cool for two minutes.

If it forms a ball without sticking to your hands it is ready. Spread the mixture into an ungreased tray.

Leave to cool and cut in pieces.

Compassionate Living the Bhumi Way

The Bhumi Project was set up in 2009 as an international Hindu response to the environmental challenges facing the planet. It is supported by all the major Hindu traditions. As well as promoting greening of Hindu temples, one of its main projects is Compassionate Living.

Hinduism has always advocated Ahimsa, or non-cruelty, as an important component of Dharma — a life centred on good thinking and right living. By personifying the Earth as Mother Bhumi, Hindu culture has built a foundation for a relationship of respect.

Step 1: Cut Out Red Meat

India's greatest epic, the Mahabharata, states, 'One should never do to another, that which one regards as injurious to one's own self. This is the rule of Dharma.' Bhumi — Mother Earth — provides for our needs generously, and Hindu thought has always recommended that we reciprocate with gratitude. By cutting out red meat from our diets, we could dramatically reduce our carbon footprint, doing the right thing by Bhumi — but also providing an example of good practice to others.

Step 2: Go Veg

Gandhi said, 'I do feel that spiritual progress does demand at some stage that we should cease to kill our fellow creatures for the satisfaction of our bodily wants.' By adopting a vegetarian diet, we can practice compassion on a greater level. Ahimsa is a development of thoughtfulness, and by abstaining from meat, fish, and eggs we can dramatically reduce the amount of resources and chemicals needed to produce our food, also reducing pollution in our environment. To go veg is to go green.

Step 3: Kind to Cows

Many of us buy milk, but are we aware of the terrible conditions in which dairy cows live? As Ranchor Prime, a Hindu environmentalist, puts it, 'milk is cheap because the lives of cows are cheap'. Cruelty-free milk is a great idea and still in its infancy. In the meantime, we can buy organic milk and dairy produce which means better welfare and conditions for animals. By continuing to buy organic dairy products, and encouraging others to do so too, we can increase the demand for cruelty-free milk.

Step 4: Buy Consciously, Buy Cruelty Free

Leather has become as common in our wardrobes as a pair of jeans, yet one billion cows are killed every year for the trade, with chemical dyes polluting rivers. You can find many good quality, non-leather alternatives on the high street and internet. Another way we can help is by buying cruelty-free health and beauty products. Millions of animals are killed in tests every year, but in a recent survey 80% of people said that they would stop buying a product if they learned that it was tested on animals.

Step 5: A Life Built on Compassion

A compassionate and thoughtful lifestyle goes beyond what we eat and the clothes we wear. It relies on an understanding of the relationship of respect between ourselves and Bhumi — Mother Earth. Hindu culture encourages us to think before we act, and remain thoughtful of the impact we have on our world and others. Our actions have consequences and we all want these consequences to make a positive contribution to the world in which we live.

The Happiest Cattle in the World

"I am the fragrance of the Earth, the heat in fire. I am the life of all that lives"

– *Lord Krishna, Bhagavad Gita 7.9*

Breakfast for the small herd of cows, calves and oxen at Bhaktivedanta Manor in Hertfordshire, Britain, is 12 kilos of organic hay.

Home is an environmentally friendly £2 million goshala (Sanskrit for cow shelter) with solar panels, underfloor heating and maternity unit.

Daily life is spent on Britain's only carbon-free working farm, where the animals are showered with love, kindness and compassion.

The Manor was given to ISKCON (the International Society for Krishna Consciousness) by George Harrison, the late Beatle, in 1973. Today it is an ashram, study centre and organic farm.

continues on page 60

the story of Gopal

Devout Hindus will go to great lengths to care for cows. This story came to us from Vrindavan Food for Life, which has a goshala (a form of protective shelter for cattle) accommodating 200 cows in Vrindavan, northern India.

Gopal is, like many others, a rescue calf, a victim of Indian traffic. These accidents are unfortunate, but not unusual.

But Gopal has a very special story to tell. He was hit by a car somewhere in the state of Gujarat and was lying injured by the roadside for days.

A woman driving by noticed the injured calf and had her driver stop.

She took the calf on her lap and drove to various goshalas, asking if they would please take care of the young bull. No one wanted him.

Then she remembered that in Vrindavan, more than 500 miles away, there was a goshala devoted to helping abandoned or injured cows, called Care for Cows.

She then bravely embarked on a 33-hour car ride to Vrindavan, carrying the calf on her lap.

Gopal is now recovering happily and securely in our Care for Cows goshala. What a journey! And what karma!

And most important, what a loving heart this woman has to undertake such trouble and inconvenience, riding for 33 hours with a calf on her lap, to save him.

– *Rupa Raghunath Das*

For Hindus, the image of Krishna as a cowherd underlines his compassion for all living creatures. Hindu tradition declares cows and bulls as sacred and in doing so protects them from abuse.

Bhaktivedanta Manor practises 'cow protection', which means the animals are not killed; they are hand-milked; calves suckle from their mothers and bulls are given work, such as ploughing and hauling.

The animals are cared for under the *ahimsa* (non-violence) philosophy, which is based on kindness towards all living beings. When an animal becomes too old to work or give milk, it is gently retired and allowed to die with dignity.

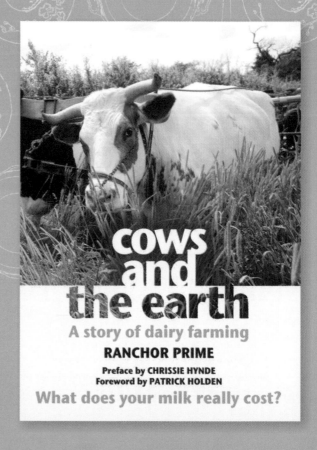

COWS and the earth
A story of dairy farming
RANCHOR PRIME
Preface by CHRISSIE HYNDE
Foreword by PATRICK HOLDEN
What does your milk really cost?

The dreamy-eyed, sleek-coated creatures are tenderly cared for by their farm workers and in 2013 the 16 dairy cows produced about 50,000 litres of cruelty-free milk. It is used in the temple's kitchens, which feeds thousands weekly, and to make the sweets or 'prasad' offered to Krishna in rituals.

In his book about the Bhaktivedanta herd, *Cows and the Earth*, Ranchor Prime says: 'Most of us are now far removed from agriculture, and as a result, we are unaware of the way farming has changed. What was once a relationship of mutual respect between humans, animals and nature, has been perverted to a regime of exploitation built upon animal slaughter. Every time we buy a product of intensive farming we are in effect buying a share in the life of an animal. The shorter and more intensely productive that animal's life, the cheaper it will be valued. On the other hand, the more we pay, the better, and possibly longer, that animal's life will be.

'Modern intensive farming reverses the four conditions of cow protection and is founded on their very opposite: Kill all animals, Use milking machines, Separate cows from their mothers, Bulls are meat.

'The alternative to this regime is to accord cows and bulls the right to life, to care for them with dignity throughout their lives, and so reap the benefits of enlightened collaboration between human and animal.'

Ahimsa milk — the campaign to end cow slavery

In May 2011 Bhaktivedanta Manor in Britain launched its Ahimsa (slaughter-free) milk as part of its movement against 'the slavery of cows in commercial milk production'. The Ahimsa Dairy Foundation's mission is 'to make slaughter-free milk a reality and establish sustainable dairy farms in Britain, which give people a real ethical choice'. The range also includes yoghurt, cheese and ghee, clarified butter.

Slaughter-free milk comes at a price. In 2013 Ahimsa milk retailed at £2.25 per litre plus £1.50 per delivery. In supermarkets the price of a 1.13 litre (two pint) bottle of whole non-organic milk was 89p. There are good reasons why Ahimsa milk is almost three times the price of mass-produced milk, says farm manager Syamasundara: 'When you produce your own milk, you start to realise how valuable milk is, and you want to use it carefully.'

The average daily yield for dairy cows in the UK is 22 litres per day, according to Compassion in World Farming. The average yield in America is even higher at more than 30 litres per day. However, these high-producing cows are productive for an average of just three years, after which they are culled for meat. By contrast, the Manor cows are productive until they are about 15 years old. They produce a daily average of 15 litres in their first year of lactation, five litres in the second and three in the third. One reason conventional cows yield more milk is that they are intensively reared by, for example, being fed large amounts of high-protein animal feed and subjected to back-to-back pregnancies. American dairy farmers also use artificial growth hormone (recombinant Bovine Growth Hormone) to increase production. This is banned in all European Union countries, as well as Canada, Australia, New Zealand, Japan and Israel, because of concerns that it substantially increases health problems in cows.

Cows at the Manor farm, on the other hand, eat mostly grass and hay, and average three years between calves. Also, at the Manor, a quarter of a cow's milk during the first six months of her life goes directly to her calf and is therefore not counted in production figures. The Manor has more than 60 cows, calves, bulls and oxen in its herd. Of these, 16 are milking cows producing about 50,000 litres per year in total. There are also 21 oxen (castrated bulls) working or being trained to work, two bulls, six retired animals and 17 others including calves, older calves, pregnant heifers or dry cows waiting their time for impregnation.

'We don't expect all our animals to be productive all of their lives,' says Syamasundara. 'We treat them as one would the members of any community, among whom both young and old have their place, whether they be children, working adults or retired. All our animals live out their natural lives. In economic terms, this means that the cost of the milk from our farm includes the cost of caring for the entire herd throughout their lives.'

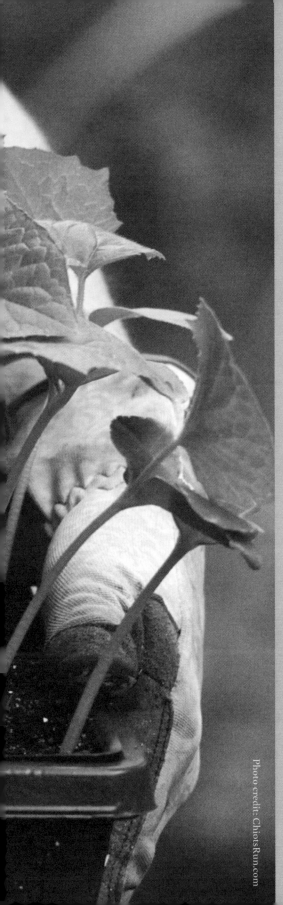

Photo credit: ChiotsRun.com

Agriculture:

The Stuff of Life

"Eat food.
Not too much.
Mostly plants."

— *Michael Pollan,*
In Defence of Food: An Eater's Manifesto

Soil is the Melting Pot of All Living Things

"The nation that destroys its soil, destroys itself"

– Franklin D. Roosevelt, 32nd American President, March 1933–April 1945

I grew up in Seoul, Korea, one of the largest mega cities in Asia and the world. When I was a child, Seoul showcased the good and bad symptoms of a rapidly industrialising economy. My pre-school years were spent playing soccer and catching bugs. Our soccer field had to be given up occasionally for trucks that honked their way through the narrow unpaved roads, and my bug-hunting ground was an abandoned field that would transition to forests if not interrupted.

Many years later in my graduate programme in America, when I found myself making my way into the science of soils and landscapes, I had a tough time answering my own question: 'What led me here?' I was jealous of those American students who claimed that their upbringing in the wilderness or rural areas helped them in choosing ecology, geology, and other environmental sciences as their careers. I did not have such humble roots.

While telling this story this year, a powerful image suddenly came back to me. It was 1975 and my grandfather had just died. I vaguely remember how he looked. No memory of his voice and any conversation with him remain with me. Since he was baptised just before he died, he was buried in a Catholic cemetery. Land is scarce in South Korea but people still die, so unploughable

and uninhabitable steep mountainsides are for the dead.

On the day of his burial, we walked up a steep hill. Graveyard workers were digging a soil pit and into it my grandfather's coffin was lowered. The soil was orange-red. I used to say that I had never seen a fully open soil pit before my graduate studies in soils. Now I take it back. I saw one, orange-red, where my grandfather was buried.

I don't remember asking my parents, 'What makes the soil orange-red?' Being a student of soil, now I have a lot to say on this question. The colour must be from mineral goethite and hematite, common kinds of iron oxides; the iron must be from the weathering of biotite; the biotite is from granitic rocks widespread in the area.

I also know that the graveyard was not occasionally flooded. It was a good pick, otherwise most microbes suffocate during the seasonal waterlogging, but few turn to breathe iron instead, which dissolves and mobilises the iron resulting in distinct visual markers. So there was plenty of oxygen that microbes took advantage of in actively decomposing my grandfather's body soundly back to Nature's nutrient cycle. A happy story indeed.

Photo credit: ARC

This newly revived memory was a relief. Why? It was difficult to explain — more precisely I felt a bit ashamed — that I had never seen a full soil profile until I decided to be an expert on the matter.

A soil profile is a face of a soil that greets you when you jump into an open pit. A soil profile has horizons — layers that systematically vary with depths.

The organic rich topsoil is called the 'A horizon'. On top of the A horizon, soils may have an O horizon that is made of fresh plant-derived materials like leaf litter. Beneath the A horizons lie the B horizons that keep what are leached out of the overlying A horizons and retain chemically and physically transformed parent material — fluvial sediments, volcanic lava, granitic rocks that could be there if not soils. The orange-red was the colour of the B horizon of the soil where my grandfather was buried.

A soil profile can have endless numbers of different looks. Arctic soils differ from temperate soils that are also distinct from tropical soils. Soils formed from volcanic ash or granitic rocks inherit some of the characters of the underlying rocks.

some soils are four million years old

In Minnesota where I live, soils under sugar maple trees are less acidic than the soils shaded by spruce. You walk up a hill and the soil on the hilltop may be dramatically different from the one at the foot of the hill. Whether you walk several steps or you fly away 5,000 miles, your feet will never step on an identical soil. There are young soils and old soils. There are still very rare soils on Earth that are four million years old.

It is more than common that people go through their entire lives without seeing

We know more about the movement of celestial bodies than about the soil underfoot.

– Leonardo da Vinci, circa 1500s

a soil profile or without noticing it even when placed right in front of their eyes. Soils are not invisible like the air we breathe. Still they don't present themselves until we put work to them and digging is hard work. Adam and Eve did not bother to labour the soil until they were destined to do so. In 1975, I was a seven-year-old with an exceptional ability to tire my parents with questions, but still was not curious enough to inquire about the soil colour. Soils offer an ultimate test of one's curiosity and very few pass.

The importance of soils cannot be taken for granted. Between rain and groundwater or stream are soils. Soil filters water, so water can only be as clean as soils. The life-protecting ozone layer high above in the stratosphere would not be there unless soils did the nitrogen cycle. Global warming — largely caused by carbon dioxide build-up in the atmosphere from fossil fuel burning — is triggering the decomposition of organic matter in arctic soils.

How much carbon is stored in the arctic soil alone? Estimates vary, but probably more than two or three times all the carbon currently in the atmosphere. We, scientists, have identified about two million biological species, but we are still scratching our heads on this question: how many different micro-

organisms can a gram of soil hold? And that one gram is likely to serve the entire Earth's known biodiversity. There is evidence that the rise of atmospheric oxygen that we breathe is tied to the co-evolution of land plants and soils in the deep geologic past.

Global population is hitting nine billion soon, and the green revolution is losing its lustre. The task of feeding these massive numbers of people may well depend on our ability to sustainably manage soils. This is a challenging job. When you plough soil, all of the processes above are seriously altered as well. There is simply no way of irrigating, fertilising, amending, adding pesticides and herbicides, and ploughing soils without dramatically disassembling and reorganising the fundamental life-supporting actions in soils. Therefore whatever we do to soils, and however we own soils, has ecological and political chain reactions simultaneously. History abundantly shows civilisations that fell because they lost their soils.

dirt is also God's creation

Hence soils are a puzzling act: groundlessly unnoticeable but heavenly crucial. The Book of Genesis in the Bible is a powerful reminder. When it describes God creating humans out of dirt, we are reminded of our humble origins. This is still true for modern men and women. We are what we eat, and it is not a joke. We have inside our bodies the element carbon. If a body weighs 70kg, it holds about 16kg of carbon that comes from carbon dioxide photosynthesised by the vegetables eaten.

This carbon went through soil countless times since the beginning of the Earth. The calcium, sodium, potassium, and phosphorus inside our bodies all came from the

did you know?

It takes 500 to 1,000 years to form an inch of soil and there are several thousand types of soil.

vegetables that took up these elements from the soils. Even if one is mostly carnivorous, the animals consumed took those elements from the vegetables they grazed on.

In Genesis, however, dirt is also God's creation that looked good to God. It is the clay-built proto-human that receives God's breath, as much as the orange-red soil that provided a resting place for my grandfather. It is precisely because the soils are a receiver that soils are a giver: we came from it and go back to it. We share this fate with other living things. Soil is the melting pot of all living things — including our own species — on the land. The proto-human was built out of this melting pot, reminding us our shared fate with other fellow living creatures.

The first soil pit that I opened with a shovel in my hands is in coastal California. It was a wet winter. On the day I went out, the rain poured and digging a soil in the middle of a storm wasn't fun. In fact, I felt miserable.

On a fine spring day, I hiked up the big hills on the other side of the floodplain. I was looking forward to a bird's eye view of my study site. It was amazing and I shouted with joy. Green hills were taking the lower half of the scene, and the rest was split between the blue Pacific Ocean and the cloudless sky. The memory from winter overlapped on the most beautiful scene. The green hills and my toil under the storm were sharing the soil that was hidden.

For the first time, I was struck by the fact that soils are buried hidden. It was the same kind of surprise that I had when my grandfather's soil came back to my memory alive.

Kyungsoo Yoo
is a soil scientist and professor
at the University of Minnesota, USA.

This article first appeared on
the **Ecojesuit** website.

*farmers watched helplessly
as their crops blew away*

The Dust Bowl is a stark reminder of what can happen when we destroy an area's ecological balance. During the 1930s, the soil literally blew away from the US and Canadian prairies, blackening the sky and reducing visibility to as little as a metre. Topsoil that had taken a thousand years per inch to build blew away in minutes.

The University of Illinois describes the despair and devastation of that time. 'For eight years dust blew on the southern plains. It came in a yellowish-brown haze from the South and in rolling walls of black from the North. The simplest acts of life — breathing, eating a meal, taking a walk — were no longer simple. Children wore dust masks to and from school, women hung wet sheets over windows in a futile attempt to stop the dirt, farmers watched helplessly as their crops blew away.'

The Dust Bowl was caused by a mixture of ignorance, poor agricultural practices and years of drought. Farmers ploughed up the arid grasslands of the prairies — often using the new mechanised farming techniques introduced in the 1920s — to plant wheat. But after years of drought, the wheat died and the native grasses that had held the soil in place was no longer there. When the winds blew, black clouds of dust filled the sky for days at a time. In many areas, three-quarters of the topsoil is estimated to have disappeared and hundreds of thousands of people were plunged into poverty.

In response, the US government introduced soil conservation methods such as ploughing in terraces and digging ditches to hold rainwater, and allowing millions of acres to lie fallow so that the soil could regenerate. Trees were planted as windbreaks in a 100-mile-wide zone across the Great Plains, and grasses were sown to anchor the soil.

Such is the miraculous power of Nature that with these strenuous efforts, by the early 1940s much of the land had been rehabilitated.

Frankenfoods or Answer to Our Prayers?

"There is no 'agricultural' reason for hunger today. Global food production has increased more quickly than population over the past half century... If people are hungry, it's because they can't afford to buy food, not that there is no food to buy"

— Patrick Love, OECD Insights blog, 2010

In the 1980s, Indian quantum physicist Dr Vandana Shiva was invited to speak at a biotechnology conference organised by the Dag Hammarskjöld Foundation. While she was there she had a conversation with a representative from the chemical firm Ciba-Geigy (which later merged to become today's biotechnology giant, Syngenta) who told her that the company's goal was to control health and food by the turn of the 21st century, and that it was going to do it by using biotechnology to change the biology of plants and animals. 'That's the day I decided I was going to start saving seeds,' Vandana says.

Since then she has founded a network of seed keepers and organic farmers in 17 states in India that offers a vision of a future free of genetically modified crops. She called it Navdanya, which means 'nine seeds'. Nine is a sacred number in India, and the name also symbolises the importance of biological and cultural diversity rather than the kind of single, controlled seed-bases that the three big biochemical giants are promoting. The issue of genetic modification (GM), sometimes called genetic engineering (GE), is one of the most contentious in modern

farming today. As proof of how bitterly this debate is fought, as this book was being finalised in late 2013, Britain's environment secretary Owen Paterson responded to a question about 'golden rice', genetically modified to tackle blindness caused by vitamin A deficiency, by saying: 'It's just disgusting that little children are allowed to go blind and die because of a hang-up by a small number of people about this technology. I think what they do is absolutely wicked.' His comments prompted outrage from many people, including a member of his own political party, Zac Goldsmith, who said: 'Commentators everywhere are wondering why high-tech golden rice should be hailed as a solution to a problem that could be solved far more cheaply and quickly with the supply of green vegetables and cheap supplements.'

So what is this 'hang-up…about this technology' all about? To their supporters, GM crops will help end world hunger and reduce the total number of pesticides needed by farmers. They argue that transgenic crops are the only way we can hope to grow enough food to feed the estimated nine billion people in the world by 2050.

Photo credit: ARC

To their opponents, GM crops violate the deepest principles of life and pose an unacceptable risk to the environment as well as human and animal health. There is a sense that humans should not be 'playing God' in this way. Opponents are also deeply troubled by the issue of who controls the technology. They see GM as the vanguard of a world food system that leaves small-holder farmers at the mercy of corporate agribusiness, and point out that just three chemical companies (Monsanto, Syngenta, and Bayer) are responsible for virtually all GM crops in the world today.

Shiva says this 'corporate control over seed' has plunged hundreds of thousands of poor farmers into debt. In the past they would store some seeds from one season and then plant them in the next. Seeds from GM crops are usually specifically designed not to be used for the following season (so farmers have to buy them each year) and in some cases also require purchase of specific pesticides, such as the Monsanto herbicide

Ready Roundup, from the big corporations. Vandana says that between 1990 and 2013 this has caused 270,000 farmers in India to commit suicide.

What's more, the technology has failed to live up to its hyperbole, says Goldsmith. 'Farmers who took on herbicide-tolerant GM crops are now struggling with the cost of combating herbicide-resistant "superweeds",' he wrote in an article for *The Guardian* in October 2013. 'Some 49% of US farms suffer from Roundup-resistant superweeds, a 50% increase on the year before. As a result, since 1996 there has been a disproportionate increase in the use of weed killers — in excess of 225 million kilograms in the US. 'Meanwhile, farmers who took on pest-resistant GM crops are struggling with the cost of secondary pests unaffected by the built-in toxins. In China and India, initial savings from reduced insecticide use with Bt cotton [a GM crop] have been eroded as secondary pests emerged.'

what are genetically modified organisms?

Genetically modified organisms (GMOs) are those in which the genetic DNA material has been altered in a way that does not occur naturally. They are also called transgenic organisms.

Biologists can select a gene from one species and insert it into another species, even if they are not related; for example a gene from a fish could be inserted into a tomato.

In this way, characteristics from one species can be transferred into another — faster growth, a specific flavour, pesticide resistance, etc.

Previously plant breeders could only create new hybrids by the time-consuming and inexact method of selective or cross-breeding species that were fairly close relatives, often over several generations, until they achieved the desired characteristics.

Other terms for GM technology include 'modern biotechnology', 'gene technology', and 'genetic engineering'.

Religious Groups and GM

Faith groups have not come to a consensus on GM crops. Some have declared there is nothing inherently wrong with genetic modification. Others have called for GM foods to be labelled, sometimes for fear that there might be a taboo transgression — for example, that Jews or Muslims may unwittingly eat vegetables produced with genes from forbidden foods such as pork — and some because they believe consumers should make their own choices.

In 2009 Emmanuel Omobowale, Peter Singer and Abdallah Daar, researchers from the University of Ibadan in Nigeria and the University of Toronto, Canada, looked at what Judaism, Christianity and Islam — followed by more than half of the world's people — said about GM.

In 'The Three Main Monotheistic Religions and GM Food Technology: An Overview of Perspectives', they found no overarching consensus in the three religions, although mainstream theology in all three 'increasingly tends towards acceptance of GM technology *per se*', albeit in a context of rigorous scientific, ethical and regulatory scrutiny and proper labelling of GM products.

Here is a summary of what they found:

Judaism

Some Jewish scholars say transgenic plants are permissible if they are not directly prohibited by God and if the research will benefit humankind. According to Jewish Rabbi Akiva Wolff, research director of the Jerusalem College of Technology's Centre for Judaism and the Environment, 'genetic engineering of animals and plants in order to save or prolong human life would certainly be permitted, if not required, by *halakhah* [Jewish law].'

Others say GM violates the Biblical prohibition of *kilayim*, or mixing of different species of animals and plants. British Jewish commentator Michael Green and US Jewish environmental group, Teva Learning Centre, say GM food is not kosher.

They cite the following Biblical verses in support of their position: 'You shall not let your cattle mate with a diverse kind; you shall not sow your field with two kinds of seed' (Leviticus 19:19) and 'You shall not sow your vineyard with two kinds of seed' (Deuteronomy 22:9–11).

Christianity

The Catholic Church is the largest Christian denomination in the world, with 1.2 billion followers. In 2003 opponents of GM were stunned when Archbishop Renato Martino, head of the Pontifical Council for Justice and Peace, came out in support of genetically modified foods, saying they could hold the answer to world starvation and malnutrition. Vatican officials accused opponents of ignoring the benefits to the world's hungry.

Velasio De Paolis, a professor of canon law at the Pontifical Urban University, said

GM messes with life, messes with truth, messes with our common inheritance, messes with justice, messes with human health, messes with the lives of peasant farmers in developing countries and the relationship between human beings and other forms of life.

— World Council of Churches

it was 'easy to say no to GM food if your stomach is full'.

In 2009 the Vatican's Pontifical Academy of Sciences held a study week after which it said GM 'used appropriately and responsibly' could 'be of major significance for resource-poor farmers'. It even went so far as to suggest there was 'a moral imperative' to bring the benefits of GM to the world's poor.

However, in 2012 a leaked US diplomatic cable revealed that despite years of pressure from American diplomats, the Vatican had resisted expressing stronger public support for GM — not because it had doubts about the technology but because of fears that it would make poor farmers dependent on rich multinational corporations. No Pope has ever pronounced on GM.

This reluctance is partly a result of internal arguments within the Church. Some Catholic groups are strongly anti-GM and believe the pro-GM lobby has infiltrated the Vatican. Groups such as the St Columban's Mission Society, an order of

Catholic priests, and Catholic bishops in the Philippines remain vigorously opposed to biotech foods.

Father Sean McDonagh, an Irish Columban priest and ecologist and an outspoken GM critic, expressed these concerns in a 2009 interview for the National Catholic Reporter newspaper. Saying he has 'a particular problem with patenting living organisms', Sean added: 'Because all genetically modified seeds are now patented, you're giving enormous control to a handful of corporations over the seeds of the staple crops of the world. It started with rice, then corn, now they're looking to wheat and potatoes. This should be totally unacceptable to anyone. Forget about the science of whether they're safe or not. To give six Western corporations, in the United States and Europe, control over the seeds of the world is outrageous.'

there's no magic bullet for hunger

Worse still, the spread of GM would increase famine and hunger, not solve it, he said: 'All the experts at Catholic development agencies have taken the position that this is not the way to address food security, and that there's no magic bullet for hunger. What's needed is land reform, financial aid to small-scale farmers, markets where they can get value so they're not caught by the "middleman". I've spent 40 years at this sort of work, and I know that's the way forward.'

These sharp disagreements are also seen in other churches. The Church of England says there is nothing inherently wrong with the principles of biotechnology but that any use of GM needs to be made within an ethical framework and with caution. The

Conference of European Churches, representing 126 churches of different Christian traditions, agrees, saying that while Nature belongs to God, it is not sacred and can be manipulated for the benefit of humankind.

However, in 2005 the World Council of Churches, a fellowship from more than 120 countries, concluded it is unethical, from a Christian perspective, for scientists to dabble in the genetic modification of food crops. Its report said GM 'messes with life, messes with truth, messes with our common inheritance, messes with justice, messes with human health, messes with the lives of peasant farmers in developing countries and the relationship between human beings and other forms of life'.

The Evangelical Lutheran Church in America endorses biotechnology in principle — but this position led one of its members, Anselm Trinity Lutheran Church, in Sheldon, North Dakota, voting to leave the ELCA in 2010. Other groups have spoken out against GM, including the Church Environmental Network in South Africa and the UK-based ecumenical group Christian Aid.

Islam

Islam's two major branches, Sunni and Shia, tend to agree on biological and technological matters. A 1998 Kuwait seminar on genetic engineering concluded that there are no laws within Islam to prevent the genetic modification of food crops and animals. However, Islamic scholars have raised concerns about the theoretical production of foods with genes from pigs.

Respected Islamic cleric Ibrahim Syed, president of Islamic Research Foundation International, says the Qur'anic verse forbidding humans from defacing God's creation 'cannot be invoked as a total and radical ban on genetic engineering... If carried too far, it would conflict with many forms of curative surgery that also entail some change in God's creation'.

In 2003, the top Muslim clerical body in Indonesia (the world's biggest Muslim country) approved the importation of genetically modified food products by Indonesian Muslims.

However, other Muslim commentators disagree. In 2007, writing on behalf of the United Kingdom Islamic Medical Association, Majid Katme said we do not have the right to manipulate anything that God has created using His divine wisdom. He said the Qur'an contains several verses prohibiting humans from tampering with God's Creation.

Striking an
Impossible Balance

"It is hazardous — and ultimately absurd, indeed sinful — to employ biotechnology without the guidance of deeply responsible ethics"

— Cardinal Peter Turkson

When Ghanaian Cardinal Peter Turkson, president of the Catholic Church's Pontifical Council for Justice and Peace, was invited to deliver the keynote address at the 2013 World Food Prize in Des Moines, Iowa, it was the trigger for the biggest volume of mail he had ever received for one event.

Letters, emails and online petitions called upon him to boycott the Prize for fear of suggesting Vatican approval of the 2013 recipients: three scientists who work at the heart of the biotechnology industry — Monsanto, Syngenta and Plant Biotechnology Outreach.

These companies were described by American commentator Jim Hightower as: 'Predatory, profiteering proliferators of expensive, genetically-altered seeds designed for crops that require large amounts of pesticides and water — the exact opposite of sustainability!'

The Cardinal huge mailbag is a sign of how controversial the whole arena of genetic modification is — and how intense the battleground for public opinion.

As Jim Hightower said: 'The biotech seed manipulator…wants the Catholic Church to bless its effort to hook poor Third World farmers on its pricey, pesticide-dependent seeds. Monsanto hopes that a World Food Prize will buff its image and impress the Vatican.'

In the end the Cardinal achieved what some might have thought impossible — standing ovations from two very different audiences.

The first came in the First United Methodist Church of Des Moines, packed with Occupy the World Food Prize protestors vehemently opposed to corporate agriculture. He was clearly moved by the stories of Iowa farmers who spoke of the abuses they had suffered at the hands of corporate agriculture.

The second standing ovation came from scientists, researchers and policymakers at the World Food Prize's luncheon. How did he appeal to such different audiences?

To everyone, the Cardinal preached the same two messages: The importance of striving for the common good rather than focusing only on profit and the need for dialogue between opposing sides.

continues on page 77

Genetic modification: the arguments **for**

🌱 For thousands of years, farmers have altered crop genetics through selective breeding; biotechnology is an extension of this well-established practice.

🌱 Biotechnology gives crops desirable characteristics (or beneficial traits) that can't be developed through breeding practices alone.

🌱 Biotechnology increases crop yields and conserves resources such as soil and water.

🌱 GMOs benefit the environment because fewer pesticides are needed.

🌱 GM crops are strictly regulated for safety and there is no credible evidence of harm to humans or animals

🌱 GM crops can benefit human health; for example, GM rice fortified with vitamin A could reduce childhood blindness in developing countries.

*Arguments taken from Monsanto (**monsanto.com**) and International Food Information Council Foundation (**foodinsight.org**).*

Genetic modification: the arguments **against**

🌱 Genetically modified organisms are made in laboratories, using totally different techniques from natural breeding methods, and pose special risks.

🌱 GMOs and their chemical inputs harm soil health, disrupt ecosystems, and reduce biodiversity.

🌱 GM corporations privatise seeds and commercialise agricultural genetic resources through patents, meaning they own these resources rather than being freely available in Nature. They aim to gain control of global food resources and lock farmers into buying inputs and costly seed.

🌱 GM supporters have been promising higher food yields for more than 20 years, without a single commercial example of this actually happening.

🌱 GM crops have increased use of weedkillers and pesticides, not reduced it, and risk developing highly resistant 'superweeds'. Some of the pesticides required for GM agriculture have been found to harm birds, insects, soil organisms, marine ecosystems and amphibians.

🌱 GM crops are not adequately regulated to ensure safety.

*Arguments taken from the Soil Association (**soilassociation.org**) and PLANT (Partners for the Land & Agricultural Needs of Traditional Peoples) (**plantpartners.org**).*

The GM battle is far from over

1. GM gives companies control and power over farmers' inputs, their seeds. We want to see farmers in control, not GM companies.

2. GM crops have been based on ideas of an over-simplistic model of the genes and how they work.

3. There is insufficient testing as to whether GM food is safe to eat—current 'substantial equivalence' testing is flawed.

4. The absence of evidence of harm from GM food does not mean that there is evidence that GM food is safe.

5. Some studies on the impact of GM diets on animals have shown negative health effects.

6. The regulations for GM crops are based not on science, but selective information provided by GM companies.

7. The claims that GM crops will solve world hunger or deliver other benefits are opinions and not evidence based science.

So what was his message when it came to transgenic plants? The findings of science can and should be used to feed the hungry, he told the WFP audience.

nature is neither sacred nor divine

'In Catholic thought, Nature is neither sacred nor divine, neither to be feared or to be revered and left untouched,' he said. 'Rather, it is a gift offered by the Creator to the human community to be entrusted to the intelligence and moral responsibility of men and women. Therefore it is legitimate for humans with the correct attitude to intervene in Nature and make modifications.'

But biotechnology also had to be subject to moral principles and values that respect the dignity of the human person and the common good. 'It is hazardous — and ultimately absurd, indeed sinful — to employ biotechnology without the guidance of deeply responsible ethics,' he said. 'There is

a need sometimes to be prudent. Let's take every reasonable measure of caution beforehand to avoid the risk to human health or the environment.'

The Cardinal's words reflect the Pontifical Academy of Sciences' position that GM can be permitted in agriculture when used morally, rightly, and for the common good. But they do not find favour with all Catholics. As environmental commentator William Patenaude wrote in his Catholic Ecology blog: 'My brothers and sisters in Christ who consider modified foods abhorrent will not be comfortable with this.'

The Cardinal ended his address with a call for conversation. 'All sides of the controversy are using many of the same key phrases such as 'overcoming hunger' and 'sustainable agriculture', thus it will only be by mutual and respectful listening, by a genuine desire to learn from the other, indeed from all the stakeholders, that the better and truly enduring sustainable solutions will be found.'

Our Planet is a Massive Desalination Unit

"Filthy water cannot be washed"

– West African Proverb

A proper understanding of the global water situation requires some familiarity with a number of fundamental issues. First of all, there is no shortage of fresh water in any global sense and water is a renewable resource. Many people are not aware of this and may be surprised.

Evaporation of water from the seas and oceans through solar heat lifts fresh water into the air, some of which then falls as precipitation on the land. This is called the hydro cycle and deposits an estimated 40,000 to 45,000 cubic kilometres of fresh water on to the Earth's land every year. Our planet can perhaps be seen as a massive desalination unit.

As the annual volume of water needed for human use worldwide — primarily drinking, washing, industry and agriculture — is an estimated 5,000 to 6,000 cubic kilometres, there is no shortage of fresh water globally speaking.

Furthermore, water is a renewable resource if we assume that the oceans and seas contain a practically limitless amount. It is sometimes stated, even by people who should know better, that we must use water carefully because as little as 3% at most of the total volume of water on our planet is fresh water, and the bulk of that water is in-accessibly locked in under the polar ice caps. This is a misleading statement.

The problem is that, for reasons of geography, climate, demography, economics and politics, not all of the available water reaches the areas where it is needed. The problem is regional and local and particularly severe where population density and poverty levels are high.

Second, the demand for fresh water on our planet is not only an issue for human beings but for Nature as a whole. Interestingly, when water issues were becoming a subject of debate and analysis in the 1980s and early 1990s, the water consumed by the natural environment was not part of the equation. It was the International Union for Conservation of Nature that rang the alarm bell at that time and, ever since, this organisation has been a strong advocate for Nature, urging the world to take care of its water needs.

Third, the United Nations set out and agreed its Millennium Development Goals in 2000, including goals for the availability of fresh, clean drinking water. Two years later, strong pressure from the NGO community led to a restatement of those goals to include the availability of water for sanitation and hygiene, factors that had been

Digging Deep for Water in Tanzania; Photo credit: ARC

overlooked in 2000 and were thus put on the agenda. In other words, it has taken some time to develop an integral approach to water issues, but it seems that we now have a fuller picture.

Whereas most regions in the Global North have learned through experience how to balance the demand for and supply of water on the basis of sound technological, economic and — more recently — ecological principles, the Global South still faces major difficulties. In Africa and Asia, close to one billion people still have insufficient access to clean drinking water and 2.5 billion people lack water for proper sanitation. Clean water for agriculture is also scarce and highly dependent on irregular rainfall, varying groundwater levels and seasonal drying up of rivers.

Water for drinking, sanitation and growing food is clearly essential for human health and hygiene. The most critical areas are where large-scale water utilities find it logistically and economically impossible to provide long-distance connections. As hundreds of millions of people in remote rural areas are

affected by this situation, any relief requires a much stronger emphasis on small-scale, affordable and sustainable local solutions with a large-scale impact. Here, the last decade has seen spectacular, yet affordable, developments. Numerous examples can be found on the websites of various initiatives in the Netherlands (see 'Useful websites' on page 230 for some of them).

The widespread availability and use of internet and mobile phone networks — particularly in the Global South — has created great opportunities to disseminate practical knowledge and experience about how to create these sustainable local solutions within communities in these countries. Such opportunities were previously almost non-existent. The challenge now is to develop these opportunities so that communities in the poorest parts of the world are no longer deprived of a commodity as essential as clean water.

Allerd Stikker is chairman of the Advisory Board of the Ecological Management Foundation, based in the Netherlands.

Where Hunger and Thirst Meet

"Say: Have ye thought: If (all) your water were to disappear into the Earth, who then could bring you gushing water?"

– Qur'an, 67:30

One in ten people across the world live without clean, safe water to drink, while two in five have nowhere safe to go to the toilet. With the global population set to exceed nine billion by 2050, pushing up the need for safe drinking water, and the predicted 70% increase in food demands placing yet more pressures on water supplies, how do we meet the ever-developing needs of a growing population?

At WaterAid, we believe the issue is not one simply of scarcity but of access, and the solution lies in ensuring access to water and sanitation for basic human needs. Furthermore, targeting the poorest communities has the greatest impact. Dirty water and inadequate sanitation have serious health implications. The World Health Organisation estimates that 50% of malnutrition is associated with repeated infections as a result of unsafe water, inadequate sanitation or insufficient hygiene. And evidence shows that under-nutrition in childhood has a lasting impact on health, education and economic prosperity.

Meanwhile, according to the UN, half the hospital beds in developing countries are filled with people suffering from diseases caused by poor water, sanitation and hygiene. This affects people's ability to farm and work, with a knock-on effect on both the availability of food and the ability to buy it.

Time is also an issue. Women and children can spend hours every day collecting water for their families. Relieving them of this burden frees up time for them to go to school and earn a living. Improved water sources close to the home can be used to irrigate household kitchen gardens, providing additional nutrition in times of food shortages, while the by-products of ecological sanitation can enhance soil fertility and crop yields.

The average Briton drinks between two and five litres of water per day and will use about 145 litres for cooking, washing and flushing. But if the embedded water used to produce the goods we consume is included, the daily use may be nearer 3,400 litres per day. Food accounts for 65% of this amount.

– Stuffed, by Pat Thomas

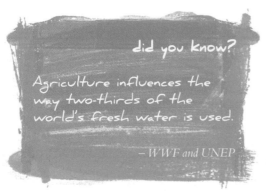

did you know?

Agriculture influences the way two-thirds of the world's fresh water is used.

— WWF and UNEP

Gaura Majhi, pictured below, is the chair of her community's water and sanitation committee in Surkhet, Nepal.

WaterAid helped install a gravity-flow water system in her village as well as ensuring all 132 households have a latrine. 'Before the system was installed, we were always sick and I would waste hours each day collecting water,' she says. 'I had to go and collect water for my family only days after giving birth. Life was tough. Now we're able to spend time on things like cultivation and as we are so close to the water supply, we can irrigate our crops.

'It's amazing to know that my grandchildren are not going to suffer in the way my children and I did.'

Barbara Frost is chief executive of WaterAid, an international charity that works to bring safe water and sanitation to the world's poorest communities.

Photo credit: WaterAid

why is the tap turned off?

Why is there water insecurity in this world? Why are 783 million people without access to safe water?

The primary problem, according to the charity WaterAid, is rarely one of physical scarcity — there IS water — but rather of socio-economic water scarcity — the water isn't being shared out evenly for political reasons, or it is being contaminated by others, or there aren't the skills to get it to where it's needed.

So, for example, in many parts of sub-Saharan Africa, South Asia, Latin America and Oceania, water resources may be present but are

not where or when they are needed most.

They may be contaminated or inaccessible because of difficult terrain. Or they may have been

did you know?

The quantity of water needed to produce one kilogram of wheat is 1,000 litres, rice, 1,400 litres, and beef, 13,000 litres.

depleted because of a lack of control over the way people take water from rivers, often for agriculture.

People and communities who are poor, or socially or politically excluded, may be ignored when national and local governments invest in extending water supply services, says WaterAid.

They may also be prevented from using existing services for social and political reasons.

Sikh Prayer

You are the Ocean of Water, and I am Your fish.

Your Name is the drop of water,
and I am a thirsty sparrowhawk.

You are my hope and You are my thirst.
My mind is absorbed in You.

Just as the baby is satisfied by drinking milk,

and the poor person is pleased by seeing wealth,

and the thirsty person is refreshed
by drinking cool water,

so is this mind drenched with delight in the Lord.

— This prayer is part of Raag Maajh, *the second raga,
or classical religious melody, in Sikhism's
holiest text, the Sri Guru Granth Sahib*

there won't always be
plenty more fish in the sea

Our seas are under immense pressure: too many fish are being taken out of the sea, too much rubbish is being thrown in and too little is being done to protect our precious marine wildlife and vital fish stocks. That's the view of growing numbers of alarmed marine biologists.

Fishing is the principal livelihood for millions of people around the world. For centuries, we have regarded the seas as an inexhaustible larder but in 1988, for the first time in human history, global wild fish catches dropped and they have continued to fall ever since. The problem is that too many boats are chasing too many fish and modern fishing technology offers vastly increased killing power to today's sophisticated mega-trawlers — multi-million-pound vessels equipped with powerful sonar systems and nets, sometimes backed up by spotter planes. And it's so wasteful. The biggest bottom trawl nets have mouths as wide as the length of a rugby field. Weighted with heavy metal rollers, they smash everything in their path as they swallow vast quantities of marine life.

Even where there are regulations, pirate fishing accounts for an estimated 20% of the world's catch and as much as 50% in some fisheries, according to the World Wildlife Fund. As a result, many fish stocks have been pushed to the point of collapse in the last 50 years. So serious is the situation that if we fail to change large-scale fishing practices now, stocks of all the fish we eat will have crashed by 2048, according to a 2006 report by an international team of ecologists and economists.

Fish farming is not an answer either, say critics such as Greenpeace, because it uses more fish than it produces due to the fact that it harvests from wild populations to feed farmed stocks. For example, 5kg of anchovies are required to farm 1kg of salmon. Greenpeace says this, plus the additional problems of pollution by fish waste and the chemicals, antibiotics and vaccines used in farmed stocks, means that in most cases fish farming only makes the problem worse.

So what can we do? The choices we make in supermarkets have a direct effect on the marine diversity of oceans and coastal fishing grounds. We need to stop buying unsustainable fish. Greenpeace and the Marine Conservation Society publish guides of species to avoid (the MCS also has a Good Fish Guide app).

The Marine Stewardship Council has developed certification schemes of sustainable fish and eco-labelling, (although some do not believe these go far enough). This has persuaded retail chains such as Waitrose or Walmart to adhere to certification when buying fish, and the fast-food chain McDonald's to use the accreditation process for its white fish. There are more than 20,000 MSC-labelled products on sale around the world, from prepared seafood meals to fresh fish from the fishmonger.

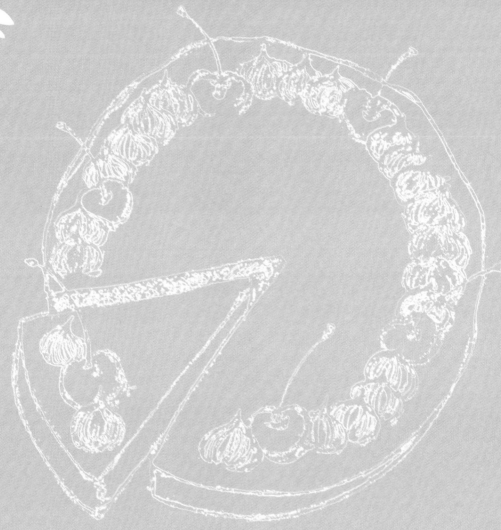

did you know?

One in three mouthfuls of the food we eat depends on pollination, mostly by the honey bee. But more than ten million beehives have been wiped out worldwide in the past six years from a mystery disease called colony collapse disorder. Campaigners blame pesticides, disease and poor nutrition.

Call to Action: Growing

- Grow some of your own food wherever you can — if you don't have a garden, use window boxes, growbags or pots.

- Get an allotment or join a community garden.

- In your garden choose plants that encourage pollinators such as bees and avoid pesticides.

- If you have spare garden space, offer it to **Landshare**, a social network connecting would-be growers with people with land, or a similar group, and let someone else get it growing.

- Plant a vegetable or fruit garden at your place of worship and encourage schools and community buildings to grow food on their land.

- Keep an eye out for wasteland in urban areas that might benefit from some guerrilla gardening. Guerrilla Gardening is a form of direct action in which gardeners plant on disused, neglected or abandoned land.

- Learn about natural methods of pest control.

- Make compost from waste food.

- Harvest rainwater and use it on your food plants.

- Pass on your surplus — don't let that good stuff go to waste!

Small changes can make big differences.

Commit to adopting one of these ideas in your daily life.

Case Study

At their own suggestion, refugees staying at Minsteracres, a Christian retreat centre in Northumberland, Britain, have worked with staff to create a Peace Garden growing fruit and vegetables in a restored Victorian walled garden.

The communal care of the garden provides a healing process for the refugees as well as learning opportunities for visiting children from inner-city communities and food for the retreat's kitchen.

Photo credit: ARC

Food and
Communities

"Yesterday is gone.

Tomorrow has
not yet come.

We have only today.
Let us begin."

– *The Blessed Teresa of Calcutta,*
best known as Mother Teresa (1910–1997)

'We are Only Three Meals away from Barbarism'

"I think we'd be very foolish to expect that we can just import everything from somewhere else and imagine that that's going to last for ever and ever and ever"

— *HRH The Prince of Wales, 2005*

There is an old Jewish saying that, if you are going to eat a chicken, first of all look after it for three days, then decide when you want to eat it.

This is perhaps a rather dramatic way of highlighting the dangers facing communities that are cut off from the actual processes of obtaining food. It reminds us to reflect upon the realities of food production.

Increasingly, even rural communities are cut off from this reality. Occasionally reality breaks through when, for example, the lambs which people have enjoyed watching gambolling in the local fields are herded on to the lorry to go to the abattoir to be slaughtered — but even then, most will turn a blind eye rather than notice them and their fate.

The industrialisation of the countryside both in the West and increasingly in other parts of the world means that we are more and more distanced from the gritty, sweaty, tough realities of food production.

How can this essential bond, with all that it means in terms of people's relationship with the methods of food production, be restored? Should it be restored? Do we gain anything from knowing more about the costs of our food?

The answer, I think, is yes we do gain more. We are less likely to waste food if we know how long it takes to produce, and what effort goes into that production. When it comes as packaged food, we have no sense of its story — its origins. If we were told how the food has come to be in our hands, we would understand that it is perhaps the product of a community of people, and that their livelihood is based upon our choices. Or that a mighty company stands between us and the farmers and that neither of us is getting the best out of the relationship. Or that we are actually dealing with a factory system where there is no more relationship with the animals than with a packet of washing powder; or the agricultural land is owned by huge corporations with no connection to communities.

This is why I think community-supported agriculture is such a good idea. Urban — but also rural but commuting communities — buy into the future production of a local farm, thereby guaranteeing the farmer has a given amount of income while we as consumers and communities share the risks and the benefits. In a good year we all do well. In a poor year the farmer survives much better than on his or her own and we take less than perhaps we had hoped for. Thus we learn again that food production should not be seen as a factory. Instead it is a gift from God and to waste or presume too much about our 'right' to have it is to run the risk of being brought up short.

But faiths are also there for the crises. They are often the very fabric of local and especially rural communities. In many rural areas of Africa or Latin America, it is the faiths that will provide schools where no one else will bother. In Indonesia, Islamic boarding schools, or *pesantrens*, are responsible for a significant proportion of rural schooling and without their input, literacy and educational opportunities would barely exist for most rural children.

In Britain, during the foot-and-mouth crisis of 2001, when millions of pigs, sheep and cattle were slaughtered in the desperate attempt to halt the spread of the disease, and when many farming families were isolated in quarantine, unable to see anyone or leave their homes, it was the faiths, especially the Church of England, which held rural communities together. As farmers' herds and flocks were taken away to be culled and burned in giant pyres, or were slaughtered on the land and buried in huge pits, it was the churches that kept those families cut off by quarantine laws from falling into despair.

It was local faithful people who called them every day. It was church congregations across Britain who raised £18 million to support the farmers and their families and helped them to rebuild their lives. And it was prayer, fellowship and community from the churches that prevented even more suicides than there were because they offered hope as well as help. William Temple, Archbishop of Canterbury during the Second World War, perhaps put better than anyone the relationship between communities, food and the land that supports the food production when he said we are 'only three meals away from barbarism'.

In a small way, this was demonstrated recently when, during a heavy snowfall in my part of England, people panicked. Although the snow was forecast to last only a few days, at some supermarkets fights broke out over the last few loaves after people had been seen buying six or seven for their own freezers.

We need to reconnect land, the realities of food and our sense of community as a preparation for when things become really difficult. Without this we will not be able to know what to do.

Martin Palmer is an author, broadcaster and Secretary General of the Alliance of Religions and Conservation (ARC).

Inspiring Story....

COMMON
PRAYER

A LITURGY
FOR ORDINARY RADICALS

'It's Easier to Get a Gun in this Neighbourhood than a Salad'

"Everybody needs beauty as well as bread, places to play in and pray in, where Nature may heal and cheer and give strength to body and soul alike"

— John Muir, Scottish-American preservationist, 1838–1914

With a smile I said, 'That's a firefly,' realising it was his first firefly sighting. 'Why does it glow like that?' I thought for a minute. 'I'm not sure. I think God just felt extra wild one day and said, "I think I'll make a bug that glows in the dark".'

'God is cool,' the kid said, grinning from ear to ear.

One of the most beautiful things we get to do here at The Simple Way is plant gardens in the concrete jungle of North Philadelphia, USA — and see kids discover the miracle of life, and fall in love with the Creator of life.

Gardens have a special place in the Christian story. After all, God first planted humanity in a garden in Eden. And the most redemptive act in history began in a garden in Gethsemane. And the story ends in Revelation with the image of the garden taking over the City of God, with the river of life flowing through the city centre and the tree of life piercing the urban concrete.

Now, as we approach 18 years of community here at The Simple Way, we have half a dozen lots that we are gardening on. And we are seeing a neighbourhood come back

to life. I will never forget the haunting words of a kid who once said years ago, 'It's easier to get a gun in our neighbourhood than it is to get a salad.' His words broke my heart. And they have continued to fan a flame all these years to try to change that reality.

When a kid pulls a carrot out of the ground for the first time, it is magical. The more they see things that are alive, the more filled with wonder they become at the God who made all this wild and wonderful stuff like fireflies and butterflies, hummingbirds and earthworms — and you and me.

loving people back to life

Sometimes it's hard to believe that there is a beautiful God when so much of what you see is ugly.

It's hard to believe in a God that is a lover of life when there is so much death and decay and abandonment. So we talk a lot these days about 'practising resurrection' — by making ugly things beautiful...and turning vacant lots into gardens...and loving people back to life. Our latest experiment in resurrection has been a new greenhouse. We built it on the fire-scorched land where our houses burned down several years ago. Now our park flaunts this solar-powered greenhouse with a 200-gallon fishpond that can hold more than 1,000 fish that will fertilise the water where plants will grow. This all adds up to an integrated system of fish-farming and hydroponics that mimics what Nature does naturally.

> Each morning we wake up on the wrong side of capitalism.
>
> But we see hope.

Building on some of the most creative techniques in urban farming, we are now cultivating life in these post-industrial ruins, where we see the dark side of the global economy every day.

Each morning we wake up on the wrong side of capitalism. But we see hope. We are building a new world in the shell of the old one. We see grass piercing concrete. We see a neighbourhood coming back to life, rising from the dead. We now have a little oasis in the 'food desert' of North Philadelphia.

In the end it's all about small things with great love. What's important to us is not how much we do, but how much love we put into doing it.

It is no coincidence that the images Jesus uses for the 'Kingdom of God' are very small. The Kingdom of God is like yeast, which you cannot even see. It's like light —

and salt — little things that have unprecedented power. And one of those images is mustard.

Mustard was an interesting metaphor. It was an invasive plant. Jews had laws against growing mustard in their gardens, because it would take over the whole garden, leaving them only with mustard. It's like the wild kudzu we have down south that can cover an entire house with greenery, or like the wild weeds that crack the foundations of our houses here in Philly. It's a beautiful and scandalous image.

Mustard is a humble plant, though — it didn't grow huge like the cedars of Lebanon, or the giant redwoods in California. Mature mustard only stands a few feet high, a modest little bush.

One thing that mustard, light, salt, yeast all have in common is that they take over — they are invasive in the best sense of the word.

Everywhere we look we see this dazzling invasion of grace in the world — spreading like wild mustard. It is happening on our block as gardens take over vacant lots. It's happening around the world as new communities sprout like seedlings.

Shane Claiborne is an activist and author, and a founding member of The Simple Way in Philadelphia, Pennsylvania, USA.

The Link between 'Local Food and Our Very Happiness'

"Only when the last tree has been cut down,
Only when the last river has been poisoned,
Only when the last fish has been caught,
Only then will you find that money cannot be eaten"

– Cree saying

There is little else in this world we need as much as food. And little else causes the same amount of environmental damage. As such, it is central to both human rights and ecological movements.

Yet, without a systemic analysis of the structural and economic influences that are shaping the production, marketing and distribution of food, we can be misled by piecemeal solutions. Many years of experience in farming cultures in both the Global North and South have shown me again and again that small-scale, diversified agriculture is the only way we can meet the food needs of our growing human population in a truly sustainable manner.

Agriculture, culture and the economy are deeply intertwined. Traditionally, stable food economies resulted from the local culture and environment-shaping agricultural practices. For many millennia before modern, mechanised agriculture, people practiced small-scale, diversified farming and provided adequately, often plentifully, for their needs.

Even today, there are still cultures where we can find these ancient systems relatively intact. I had such an experience when I first went to Ladakh or 'Little Tibet', in northern India, in the 1970s. There I found that the people provided for themselves through subsistence farming, but it was far from the scenes of drudgery and near starvation that often come to mind when we hear the word subsistence. The Ladakhis' Buddhist traditions provided a constant reminder of the inextricable interdependence of all forms of life. And their profound respect for other life forms contributed to farming practices that sustained their lives for centuries.

tasks were accompanied by mantras and songs

Despite the extreme climate of the Himalayas and a scarcity of resources, Ladakhis achieved not only self-sufficiency, but frequently had surplus to trade for salt, jewels and metals. This appeared all the more remarkable since people had only the most basic tools to work with: plough, spades, saws, sickles, and hammers. For many tasks in which we would employ large machinery, Ladakhis had animals and teamwork instead, each task accompanied by mantras and song.

Photo credit: Prayudi Hartono

Three decades of development since, however, have led to a number of fundamental changes in Ladakh, perhaps the most important of which is the fact that people are now dependent on food from thousands of miles away. The end result of this long-distance transport of subsidised goods is that Ladakh's local economy has been steadily dismantled, and with it the local community that was once tied together by bonds of interdependence.

The result has been growing insecurity and competitiveness — even ethnic conflict — among a once secure and cooperative people. A range of related social problems has appeared almost overnight, including crime, breakdown of the family and homelessness. And as the Ladakhis have become separated from the land, their awareness of the limits of local resources has dimmed. Pollution is on the increase, and the population is growing at unsustainable rates.

local food to feed the world

It is clear from the example of Ladakh that food lies at the crossroads of economy, culture and the environment. Furthermore, we see that globalising the food economy has knock-on effects that can touch every aspect of life. If development is needed, in the food system or elsewhere, localisation will be a far better strategy for economic stability, cultural harmony and sustainability.

In general, Ladakhis worked hard for only four months of the year. In the eight winter months, they cooked, fed the animals, and carried water, but work was minimal. Most of the winter was spent at festivals and parties. Even during summer, hardly a week passed without a festival or celebration of one sort or another, while in winter the celebration was almost nonstop.

There is a widespread misunderstanding that we need large-scale agriculture to feed the growing human population. This has led to us accept ever-increasing monocultures, which demand enormous inputs of water, pesticides and fertilisers. Genetically modified crops are introduced under false promises of increased yields and export-oriented production is part of so-called development. From this standpoint, it appears as if feeding the world's population is at odds with environmental protection and sustainability.

localised systems actually produce more food

However, stepping back to look at the bigger picture, we see that the global system is propped up by a whole range of subsidies, regulations and heavily biased trade treaties, with one eye on perpetually increasing gross domestic product (GDP).

Understanding these mechanisms can help us shift the overall economy towards supporting small-scale on a large scale — a shift that would create a cascade of economic, social, ecological and health benefits.

Local food is, simply, food produced for local and regional consumption. For that reason, 'food miles' are relatively small, which greatly reduces fossil fuel use and pollution. It does not mean eliminating all trade. We can still eat oranges in northern climes and exotic spices can still traverse the globe. What it does mean is sourcing your food from as close to home as possible.

If apples can be produced in your region, that is where they should come from. And instead of flying them 3,000 miles away to be washed, waxed and boxed by sweatshop workers, only for the apples to appear later in your neighbourhood supermarket, we need to be able to buy them direct from the orchard or a local grocer.

In this age of impending oil shortages and global climate change, it is sheer madness to waste fossil fuels transporting food needlessly around the planet.

Local markets give farmers an incentive to diversify, which creates many niches on the farm for wild plant and animal species. Diversified farms cannot accommodate the heavy machinery used in monocultures, thereby eliminating a major cause of soil erosion. Diversification also lends itself better to organic methods, since crops are far less susceptible to pest infestations.

Since most of the money spent on food goes to the farmer, not corporate middlemen, farming will become a genuine livelihood again. Small, diversified farms can help reinvigorate entire rural economies, since they employ far more people per acre than large monocultures. Wages paid to farm workers benefit local economies and communities far more than money paid for heavy equipment and the fuel to run it: the latter is almost immediately siphoned off to equipment manufacturers and oil companies, while wages paid to workers are spent locally.

Contrary to popular belief, localised systems actually produce more food and could more effectively reduce endemic hunger than any current globalised strategies. Studies carried out all over the world have shown that small-scale, diversified farms actually have a higher total output per unit of land than large-scale monocultures.

Not only can localised food systems provide for our global food needs, they can do so while protecting the environment and providing a centrepiece for the entire local economy. We know that strong local economies provide a foundation for healthy communities, which in turn foster

the distorting impact of money

When tourism first began in Ladakh in 1975, it was as though people from another planet suddenly descended on the region. Each day many tourists would spend as much as $100 — roughly equivalent to someone spending $50,000 a day in America. In the traditional subsistence economy, money played a minor role, and was used primarily for luxuries. Basic needs — food, clothing and shelter — were provided for without money. The labour one needed was free of charge, part of an intricate web of human relationships.

Ladakhis did not realise that money played a completely different role for the foreigners, that back home they needed it to survive, that food, clothing and shelter all cost money. Compared to these strangers, they suddenly felt poor.

This new attitude contrasted dramatically with the Ladakhis' earlier self-confidence. In 1975, I was shown around the remote village of Hemis Shukpachan by a young Ladakhi named Tsewang. It seemed to me that all the houses were especially large and beautiful. I asked Tsewang to show me the houses where the poor people lived. Tsewang looked perplexed a moment, then responded, 'We don't have any poor people here.' Eight years later I overheard Tsewang talking to some tourists. 'If you could only help us Ladakhis,' he was saying, 'we're so poor.'

– localfutures.org

psychological wellbeing. Thus, there is a direct link between local food and our very happiness.

There is already a vibrant local food movement at the grassroots level with thousands of initiatives around the world. Without policy shifts, however, these projects are likely to remain isolated and ineffective on a global scale. We need to raise awareness to create a strong movement for policy change. Rebuilding local food economies is not about ending international trade, but it's about shifting the subsidies and supports for large-scale monocultures, for chemical and industrial farming, and globalised food trade.

International faith groups, who are working for the welfare of people, are ideally placed to aid in this movement. Localising food economies is a matter of ethics; it's about human rights. Shifting towards the local is an essential step towards protecting both cultural and biological diversity, and building economies that ensure a liveable future for people and the planet.

Author and filmmaker
Helena Norberg-Hodge is director of the International Society for Ecology and Culture (ISEC), a pioneer of the worldwide localisation movement.

Helena was presented with the Right Livelihood Award (known as the Alternative Nobel Prize) in the Swedish Parliament in 1986, and the Goi Peace Prize in 2012.

Chicago's
Garden of Eden

KAM Isaiah Israel is one of the oldest Reform synagogues in Midwest America, located in Chicago. Five years ago, the congregation transformed its front lawn into an urban farm. Today, it is Chicago's largest donor of farm fresh harvest grown within the city limits, which it donates to soup kitchens and shelters. The Chicago Jewish News calls it 'Chicago's Garden of Eden'.

'To date we have harvested and delivered over 12,000 pounds (around 5.4 tonnes) of food, most of which was grown on site at three urban houses of worship,' says the synagogue's president, Robert Nevel. 'A big part of our programme involves transforming urban congregational lawns into food-producing, mini farms.'

Three times a week during the growing season, workers from the congregation and the community tend and harvest the synagogue's three gardens. They hold an annual weekend every January devoted to discussing issues of food justice and the environment and run a Food Justice and Sustainability Young Leadership summer programme for teenagers.

'The urban farm unites people across generations. On any given day I could see a three-year-old farming next to an 83-year-old,' Robert says.

Great Idea!

Love is:
A Growth Industry...

Soups, stews and salads are being provided for the poor and hungry all year round, thanks to Sister Jeremias Stinson and Sister Grace Ellen Urban and their highly productive polytunnels.

For the past four years Sr Jeremias and Sr Grace Ellen have been growing armfuls of fresh produce to boost the kitchens of the Helping Hands Of St Louis Parish soup kitchen in north-west Ohio, USA.

'Hunger is a 12-month problem, but here in Ohio, the freeze hits in October and nothing grows till summer,' Sr Jeremias, pictured behind Sr Grace, said.

Great Idea!

Paul Cook, Helping Hands director, said the food donations are significant to St. Louis' impoverished guests. 'When you're living on $1,400 a month, the money doesn't stretch far enough to buy fresh tomatoes, lettuces and apples,' he said.

The word is spreading about their technique for growing vegetables year-round in a climate that is not suited for it and they are helping local and state organisations learn how to replicate it.

The year-round garden is just one of the Sisters' many duties. They are also in charge of environmental stewardship, shrines and woodland management for the Sisters of St Francis of Sylvania headquarters.

Produce Locally, Consume Locally

"Even in a single leaf of a tree or a tender blade of grass, the awe-inspiring Deity manifests itself"

– 8th-century Shinto poet

The perception of Nature in the East, especially Japan, is very different from that of the West. To the Japanese, Nature encompasses all the laws and phenomena that exist in the universe.

Life, human beings and the four seasons are all examples of these phenomena. This differs sharply from the West's scientific, analytical view of Nature.

During each season we experience a different aspect of Nature's bounty. In spring we enjoy the beauty of cherry blossoms and in autumn the changing colour of the foliage. The heat of summer and coldness of winter represent Nature's extremes. The universal laws of Nature are manifest in these phenomena and affect our everyday experience. The Japanese find it difficult to differentiate between humanity and Nature; they are seen as indivisible.

This belief is at the root of Japanese religious ideas and the basis of spiritual values since ancient times. Japanese religion rests on a model that is in harmony with the laws of Nature. The Japanese see God in natural phenomena. They pray to the Sun, show gratitude to rain and believe that gods are present in what in Western eyes would seem inanimate objects. The Japanese

respect the feeling that humanity lives due to the blessings of Nature.

Over the past century Japan has undergone increased westernisation leading to industrialisation and the emergence of a more materialistic lifestyle. The result has been confusion in various aspects of life, and degradation in the intrinsic quality of life. The reconstruction of the nation from the state of ruin following its defeat in the Second World War gave rise to materialism. This has led to spectacular economic growth but has created a deep imbalance with respect to spiritual values.

More than half a century ago, Mokichi Okada (1882–1955), founder of MOA (Mokichi Okada Cultural Services Association), foresaw this predicament. He anticipated the need for both spiritual and materialistic components in order to create a harmonious civilisation. He believed that the key to our future existence was to achieve a balance to prevent materialism from overpowering the spiritual side.

Okada thought that the existence of the spirit is at the centre of all natural phenomena; the combination of spiritual elements; fire, water and earth provide the basis for all universal objects.

Photo credit: MOA

creased consumption. By uniting farmers who implement nature farming we have established production co-operatives. The co-operatives rationalise distribution costs and produce high-quality grains, vegetables and fruits. Today in Japan there are more than 2,000 commercial farmers actively involved and nearly 300 co-operatives established throughout the country.

We live in different times from those of our founder Mokichi Okada. Generations of chemical farming have weakened the Earth's strength to produce, and there is the terrible danger of chemical pollution of underground water reservoirs and atmosphere.

The relationship between food consumption and health is quite clear. The ill effects of much of today's popular diet are manifested in the diseases afflicting our population. At the same time there is a growing awareness that natural foods can be beneficial for those suffering from various allergies and skin disorders.

Today voices around the world call for effective, safe farming methods that will outperform chemical farming. At MOA we feel our mission is to pave the way for new agriculture. Towards this goal we are exploring how to increase the quality and productivity of nature farming methods and their positive benefits for humanity.

What this means to agriculture is that it is ideal to produce agricultural produce using the Earth's power and in a state that is as close to Nature as possible. He termed this 'nature farming'. Nature farming supports the philosophy of *chisan chisho* — 'produce locally, consume locally' — a key concept that promotes self-sufficiency in our ability to feed ourselves.

In Japan, MOA is expanding awareness of Okada's nature farming produce and is generating wider distribution and in-

Dr Shoji Mizuno is executive director of MOA Nature Farming & Culture Agency, Japan.

The Proof is in the Pudding

The Food for Life Partnership is a campaign to transform food culture in British schools by bringing pupils, teachers and the wider community together to enjoy good, wholesome food.

Schools on the programme are growing their own food, organising trips to farms, sourcing food from local bakers, butchers and farmers, providing cooking and growing clubs for pupils and their families, and serving freshly prepared, locally sourced meals that follow a rigorous Food for Life Catering Mark.

'Food, glorious food' could be the motto of a primary school nestling in the Somerset town of Midsomer Norton in south-west England. St John's Church of England Primary School is a flagship school in the Soil Association's Food For Life Partnership. And today, as proud bearers of the first Gold Award, pupils, parents and teachers are all enjoying the fruits — and veg — of their labours.

As head teacher Carolyn Banfield explains: 'The main motivation was to teach the children about food and nutrition. If you asked them where a potato came from they would tell you "Sainsbury's". We had been trying to teach them about eating fresh, healthy food but it wasn't really working because we were doing it more in theory than in practice.'

Today, the 379 pupils aged between four and 11 grow organic food in raised beds and a polytunnel. Produce is incorporated into the lunch menu and surplus is sold through a farmers' market to raise money for seeds. Large compost bins are used to convert vegetable waste from school dinners into eco-friendly plant food that is dug back into the raised beds.

The fruit and vegetables are prepared and cooked in the school's sparkling £200,000 cookery room, which was opened by celebrated chef and baker Richard Bertinet in 2011. A weekly after-school cookery club meets there and parents and children can prepare a recipe — and then take it home to eat.

School business manager Jacqui Flower said: 'Food For Life really gets the children fired up and brings many subjects together.

'They are involved with growing things, then cooking them and learning about weighing and mixing. It is all part of the curriculum. Since we opened the new cookery room, people come in and say, "Wow! They don't even have this at secondary school".'

The school has even gone so far as renaming their dining hall Purple Planet, replacing the plastic airline trays with proper crockery and cutlery and having music in the background — just like in a real restaurant.

Year 5 and 6 pupils (nine to 11 year olds) apply for positions as Happy Lunchtime Helpers and their duties include helping the younger ones with their lunch.

It's a proper job: when a vacancy arises it is advertised on the school notice board and pupils are invited to fill in an application form. Candidates are then interviewed and the lucky ones who land a job are paid in house points.

Carolyn Banfield added: 'Our food culture has changed dramatically and the children's influence on their parents has been great. Lots of them now have allotments or grow their own at home.

'To get the Gold Award in 2009 and 2011 really was the icing on the cake but what's really important is teaching children important life skills. There have been huge difficulties along the way, but everyone is committed and everyone is enjoying it.

'Most of all, I am incredibly proud of the children. The way they spoke in front of the Food For Life Gold Award assessors was very professional and convincing. I am amazed at what a wonderful understanding they now have, and how good they are at articulating it.

'When the school first started the cooking classes, many parents didn't actually know how to cook. Now they have realised it's a great way of spending quality time with their children and that cooking good food from scratch is easier and cheaper than buying ready-made meals.'

And as one pupil said: 'My mum couldn't bake before and now she bakes a lot better.' The proof of the success of St John's Church of England School and the Food For Life Partnership is certainly in the pudding.

More than 4,500 schools have enrolled in Food for Life and the benefits go further than simply improving school meals, says the Food for Life Partnership.

An impact study found twice as many primary schools received an 'outstanding' rating after working with Food for Life, and 45% of parents said they were eating more vegetables as a result of the programme.

what do Food for Life pupils eat?

Schools in the Food for Life Partnership work towards the following awards:

**Bronze schools
serve meals with:**

- No undesirable food additives, hydrogenated fats or GM ingredients.

- 75% of meals freshly prepared.

- Meat that meets British welfare standards and eggs from cage-free hens.

- Seasonal menus.

- Well-trained catering staff.

**Silver schools do
all this plus offer:**

- A range of local, organic and fair trade food.

- High welfare chicken, eggs and pork products (at least Freedom food or free-range).

- No fish from the Marine Conservation Society 'fish to avoid' list.

- Display information on where the food has come from.

**Gold schools do all
this plus offer:**

- At least 30% of ingredients organic or Marine Stewardship Council certified.

- At least 50% of ingredients locally sourced.

- Organic meat, dairy products and eggs with a welfare gold standard.

- Non-meat dishes are promoted as part of a healthy, balanced, climate-friendly diet.

Inspiring Story...

Great Idea!

Making a World of Difference

In 2007 the United Nations asked the Alliance of Religions and Conservation (ARC) to invite the faiths to consider how they could help protect the environment.

In November 2009, 31 faith traditions — including Baha'ism, Buddhism, Christianity, Daoism, Hinduism, Judaism, Islam, Shintoism and Sikhism — launched long-term environmental action plans at the Many Heavens One Earth event at Windsor Castle, hosted by Prince Philip and the United Nations Secretary-General Ban Ki-moon.

Deputy UN Secretary-General Olav Kjörven described it as 'potentially the biggest civil society movement on climate change in history'. Here are some examples of their pledges around food and farming.

The Daoists reaffirmed the ban issued in 2000 on ingredients from endangered animals and plants in food and Traditional Chinese Medicine (TCM). Daoism is the cultural, philosophical, religious and physiological basis for Traditional Chinese Medicine, so this is significant. They also pledged to set up health-maintenance centres within Daoist temples to provide food therapy, medicine therapy and healthcare programmes, and to run these in an environmentally friendly way.

The Jewish plan included a goal for the Jewish community to reduce its communal meat intake by half within six years. The plan says: 'We now know that it is only possible to eat large quantities of affordable, cheap, kosher meat if the animals that are consumed are industrially raised in ways that cause them suffering throughout their lives and at their deaths.'

The Shanghai Buddhists recommended that Buddhist-owned restaurants do not serve meat from wild animals, and urge their followers to adopt a more vegetarian diet, to protect the environment.

Sikh gurdwaras, or temples, feed an estimated 30 million people every day around the world with free vegetarian food. The Sikh plan pledged to look at ways of sourcing more sustainable fuel for their communal kitchens and also asked gurdwaras to use reusable cups and plates, or ones made out of compostable material, as well as to buy locally grown and/or organic foods.

The Muslim long-term plan included a proposal to introduce Islamic eco-labelling for goods, services and foods that are ethical, environmentally friendly and faith-consistent for use throughout the global Muslim community of 1.4 billion people.

The Presbyterian Church in Cameroon runs a rural development agricultural programme. As part of its Seven-Year Plan, it committed to introducing courses on modern food crop and livestock practices for communities, and training farmers in sustainable agricultural systems, including biological methods of fertilising the soil. The Polish Autocephalous Orthodox Church has set up a new food regime in its Suprasl Academy to ensure that more than 70% of ingredients in the refectory kitchen are fresh, local and organic. This is part of a wider plan to promote organic farming in Podlasie Region in eastern Poland — considered the 'green lungs of the country'. The Northern Diocese of the Evangelical Lutheran Church of Tanzania is discouraging packaged, processed foods and promoting fresh foods instead. It is also popularising the use of compost and manure from livestock rather than chemical fertilisers 'which, in the long term, kill the soil'.

Windsor Castle's vegan banquet

Nine faiths, nine food traditions, dozens of different nationalities, one royal banquet...and one royal prince. Some people required halal food, others kosher, and still more vegetarian. Some people couldn't consume alcohol or eat onions or garlic for religious reasons, and all of them needed food that was ethical, faith-consistent and environmentally friendly.

That was the chef's nightmare when it came to designing the menu for ARC's Many Heavens, One Earth Celebration hosted by HRH The Duke of Edinburgh. The result? The first ever vegan banquet to be served at Windsor Castle. Here is the groundbreaking menu, of which more than half was locally sourced and organic.

Starter

Salad of roasted English pear, steamed celeriac and oven-roasted cobnuts nestling on frisée leaves tossed with a hazelnut oil and lemon oil dressing and served with a red grape reduction;
Ciabatta bread served with olive oil

Main course

Portobello mushroom stuffed with artichoke, red onion and thyme, set on pearl barley and butternut squash risotto with gremolata oil;
Roasted carrots, parsnips and beetroot turned with baby chard

Drinks

Cranberry and fresh orange cocktail;
Jugs of iced tap water and lemon on the tables;
Organic wines by
Le Monastère de Solan

Sharing Wisdom, Prayer — and Organic Wine

The descriptions of the wines produced by Le Monastère de Solan in the south of France sound as if they are being recited from a book of poetry. 'A rich, rare, sweet wine…sugar and aromas drying for several months by the mistral…a pale yellow robe…a gorgeous ruby red colour with a deep purple tinge…an aroma of pepper, coffee and blackberry…reinforced with leather notes…'

These lovingly created organic wines were served at the Many Heavens, One Earth banquet and celebration organised by the Alliance of Religions and Conservation (ARC) at Windsor Castle near London in November 2009, where 31 long-term commitments to environmental action were launched by nine major faiths worldwide.

The vines are tended by the 18 nuns and lay members, led by Mother Hypandia. In addition to wine, the monastery produces organic fruit and vegetables, jams and olive oil. Friends of the Monastère share their expertise through agroecology workshops. ARC has been a partner in developing the monastery's organic programme for more than ten years as part of its environmentally friendly farming programme.

Food and Worship in Judaism

"We praise You, G-d, Ruler of the universe, who sustains the entire world with goodness, kindness and mercy. G-d gives food to all creatures, for G-d's love is everlasting.

Through G-d's abundant goodness we have never been in want; may we never be in want of sustenance for the sake of G-d's great Name.

G-d sustains all, does good to all, and provides food for all of the creatures which G-d has created.

We praise You, G-d, Who provides food for all."

— *A traditional Jewish grace after meals*

Photo credit: Hazon

Food is
Memory, Family and Culture

"Even if I knew that I would die tomorrow, I would still plant an apple tree today"

– Rabbi Hillel

I'm writing this on the eve of Yom Kippur, the fast day that is the holiest day of the Jewish calendar. It's an appropriate moment to reflect on the centrality of food in Jewish life, and on the multiple ways that our relationship to food shapes who we are and how we influence the world.

I want to sketch out some of the vital elements of the traditional Jewish relationship to food, how they're evolving today, and what we all might learn from them.

It's an important task because religions are no longer islands unto themselves. Our communities need to stand not only for their highest ideals — which sometimes run the risk of sounding like platitudes — but also to be challenged by the tougher questions: how do your ideals play out in reality? Do they have meaning in the 21st century? Can they really help us live better lives, in all senses, and if so, how?

Jewish tradition — a maximalist tradition — makes sweeping demands on observant Jews in relation to food. It defines what is and isn't *kosher* — literally 'fit' — to eat. It mandates that we rest one day in seven (Shabbat is the Jewish day of rest) and on that day, share joyous meals with friends and family. It requires that we make daily ongoing provision to feed the poor; that we rest the land, one year in seven; and that we treat our animals consistently well. There's a specific religious obligation, for instance, to feed your animals on fast days. It demands that we not eat thoughtlessly, but first pause to make a *bracha*, a blessing, both before and after eating.

These obligations are taken seriously. I keep kosher. I say food *brachot* (blessings). I keep Shabbat. Like any religious tradition, it's possible to observe these things unconsciously, unmindfully, simply by rote. But the lessons of Jewish tradition have their own cumulative impact. It's entirely possible to be Jewish and to eat badly — again, in all senses. But the grain of the tradition exerts a considerable force towards eating mindfully and eating well.

> Without sustenance, there is no Torah. Without Torah, there is no sustenance.
>
> *– Pirkei Avot 3:21*

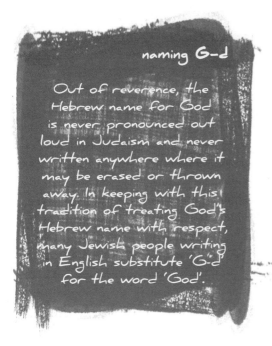

naming G-d

Out of reverence, the Hebrew name for God is never pronounced out loud in Judaism and never written anywhere where it may be erased or thrown away. In keeping with this tradition of treating God's Hebrew name with respect, many Jewish people writing in English substitute 'G-d' for the word 'God'.

That's why, I think, the contemporary Jewish Food Movement has so much momentum.

Hazon now has the largest faith-based Community-Supported Agriculture (CSA) system in the United States — nearly 10,000 Jewish people supporting 48 different farms, creating more than 170 discrete educational events, and giving more than 40,000 lbs of produce to people in need.

Jewish farming programmes are sprouting. New ethical kosher food businesses are developing. Jewish institutions are using Hazon's Food Guide to address food in systematic ways: what food do we serve after services and at celebrations? Do we serve soda or use plastic bottles? What are the trade-offs between communal norms and individual freedoms? Where does our meat come from? Should we serve it at all? Do we grow any of our own food? Do we compost our leftovers? What about food justice? What about interfaith issues? The *shmita*

(sabbatical) year takes place in 2014–2015: how can or could or should our relationship to food be different in the *shmita* year?

The Jewish community is famously fractured: two Jews, three opinions. But when I step back, and when I talk to religious leaders in other communities, I understand both that Jews have no monopoly on wisdom and — at the same time — that we actually do have much to teach in relation to food. Today all of us, in some sense, are asking: is this food kosher? Is it fit for me to eat? The lesson of Jewish tradition is that these are good questions, and they require an ongoing religious framework to help support the evolution of practice and behaviour. They should be taken seriously; and genuinely as questions, not as answers. Education leads to action. Habits change slowly. Food is not just ethics and religion but also memory, family, culture. And appetite in all senses.

So as I prepare for the start of the Yom Kippur fast, I end with this: may each of us be blessed to eat thoughtfully; to be generous with ourselves and with others; and thus to create a healthier and more sustainable world for all.

Nigel Savage is president of Hazon (Hebrew for 'vision'), a non-profit organisation that works to create healthier and more sustainable communities.

It has produced a food guide on ethical eating for Jews.

The New Jewish Food Movement

Over the past few years, a growing number of Jewish foodies, farmers, rabbis, chefs and others have been asking why and how they can eat in a way that is both deeply Jewish and deeply sustainable. As one observer commented: 'There are passionate debates over *kashrut* (the system of Jewish dietary laws) and the ethical treatment of animals, from protesting violators to developing humanely treated kosher chickens. There are new delis creating locally sourced, hand-crafted traditional foods like smoked meat...

'There are foragers interested in the connection between Biblical wandering and wild foods. There are Jewish farms and farmers in North America finding new value in following Jewish law in farming practices in sowing and reaping.'

This ferment of conversation and action — dubbed the New Jewish Food Movement — is leading Jews to think more broadly and deeply about their food choices to include environmental considerations as well as what is kosher. It is about Jews growing more of their own food and eating healthily but it is also about social justice and about understanding that food is a right — not a privilege — and that everyone should have access to fresh food and control over their own food systems.

The American Jewish food and environment movement Hazon has been at the forefront of these discussions. In 2008, its food conference unveiled a set of draft seven-year goals with the aim of achieving its vision of an American Jewish community that is not only itself healthier and more sustainable but also playing a bigger role in making the world healthier and more sustainable for all. At the core of this vision is the idea that Jewish life will be strengthened and renewed by the work of the Jewish food movement.

To that end, Hazon has been forging strong relationships between farms, farmers and Jewish communities through its community supported agriculture network as well as working to make Jewish food education a discrete discipline and promoting a reduction in meat-eating within the Jewish community.

Hazon has also produced a 130-page guide, *Food for Thought: Hazon's Sourcebook on Jews, Food & Contemporary Life.* It begins by asking the question: 'How do we live sustainably in the Age of Awareness — an age in which we're profoundly aware of how we're damaging the planet on which we live?' *Food for Thought* looks at Jewish sacred texts on food through fresh eyes, applying traditional Jewish wisdom to a range of contemporary issues to help readers think more critically about the food they eat.

Photo credit: Hazon

Jewish Dietary Rules

"Blessed art thou, O Lord my G-d, King of the universe, who brings forth the bread from the Earth"

— Hamotzi (the Jewish blessing over bread)

There are more than 13 million Jews in the world, more than five million of whom live in Israel. Food and Jewish religious life are deeply entwined, with a strict system of *kashrut*, or dietary laws, that govern which foods are considered kosher — meaning 'fit, or proper for use' — for Jews to eat. Jews follow the dietary laws to show their obedience to God.

The laws are very specific. For example, the Torah (the Hebrew Bible) states in Leviticus, chapter 11, 'Any animal that has a cloven hoof that is completely split into double hooves, and which brings up its cud, that one you may eat.' So kosher meat must come from animals that fit this description — for example, cows and goats rather than pigs. Kosher poultry includes duck, chicken, goose and turkey, and kosher fish includes only species with fins and scales.

Animals must have been slaughtered according to Jewish law to be considered kosher; the animal must be killed 'with respect and compassion', using a very sharp knife, by a qualified slaughterer. Certain fats and sinews are forbidden, and the meat is salted to remove all traces of blood.

Other rules include never eating meat and milk in the same meal; different pots, crockery, cutlery and washing-up equipment are used for dairy food, and Jews must wait for three hours after they've eaten meat or fowl before they can have dairy food, even a cup of tea.

Food plays a major role in all Jewish religious festivals, although the specific foods used may differ nationally. Fasting is also part of Jewish observance to atone for sins or make special requests to God. On complete fast days, for example, Yom Kippur (the Day of Atonement), eating and drinking are forbidden from sundown to sundown. Partial fast days mean no food or water from sunrise to sunset.

an all-embracing blessing

Intention, especially around food, has always been a foundation of Jewish life. The sages created a system of blessings that appreciates the differentiation in the species of the world. There is a blessing for the fruit of the vine, the fruit of the earth, the fruit of the tree.

At the top of the hierarchy, the blessing that can apply to all food, is our blessing for bread, **Hamotzi**. Why is bread the food that encompasses all categories? Because bread demands both wheat from the Earth and a complex process once harvested. The **Motzi** is as much a blessing for a partnership between humans and God.

— Congregation Rodeph Shalom, a Reform congregation in Philadelphia, USA

Jewish Festival Food

Passover: Passover (Pesach in Hebrew) is one of the most important festivals in the Jewish year. It commemorates the emancipation of the Israelites from slavery in ancient Egypt more than 3,000 years ago. The story can be found in the Book of Exodus, Chapter 12 in the Torah, the Hebrew Bible.

Passover is also known as the Festival of the Unleavened Bread and begins with the Seder — a ritual feast that means 'order' in Hebrew. It involves 14 steps and foods are used as symbols to help faithful Jews remember the story of the Israelites escaping Egyptian slavery, told in the Biblical book of Exodus. Dry unleavened bread, called matzo, is served to remember that when the Pharaoh allowed the Israelites to flee, there was no time to allow loaves of bread to rise.

During the whole of Passover, faithful Jews abstain from any form of leavened food products, finding imaginative ways to make 'Passover cakes' using potato starch or matzo flour instead of wheat flour. Matzo balls are little dumplings made from matzo meal bound together with eggs and oil or chicken fat. Families have their own treasured recipes, some people like their matzo balls light and fluffy, others prefer a denser, more filling consistency.

Matzo Balls

Ingredients

(Use planet friendly, fairly traded, free-range ingredients wherever possible.)

Makes 12 to 15 matzo balls

4 eggs

120ml / 4fl oz / half cup soda water

2 tbsp vegetable oil or chicken fat (schmaltz)

2 tbsp finely chopped parsley

30g / one and a quarter oz ground almonds or walnuts

1 tsp of almond or walnut oil 4 or 5 scrapes of freshly grated nutmeg

Salt

Freshly ground black pepper

125g / 4 and a half oz matzo meal

Method

Whisk the eggs until blended. Add the soda water, vegetable oil or chicken fat, salt (sparingly) and pepper. Blend in the parsley, almonds or walnuts, almond or walnut oil, nutmeg, and matzo meal. Cover and refrigerate for about one hour.

Bring a large saucepan of salted water to the boil. Rub a little oil on your hands and form matzo balls with about two tablespoons of mixture. Drop in boiling water and simmer covered for about 25 to 35 minutes. The matzo balls are often served in a chicken broth.

Potato Latkes

Hanukkah: In the 2nd century BC, the Seleucid Empire, which ruled over the land that is now Palestine and Israel, ruled that Jewish religious practice was forbidden. A small band of Jewish dissidents, known as the Maccabees, from the Hebrew word for hammer, rebelled against this edict. Today, every year, Jews around the world celebrate their victory and rededication of the holy Temple in Jerusalem, with Hanukkah, the Jewish Festival of Lights. According to Rabbinic tradition, the Maccabees could only find a small jug of oil suitable for their ceremony. It should have been enough to keep the Menorah candles burning for a single day, but instead it lasted for eight, when they could get more supplies. The traditional Hanukkah food of latkes, or fried potato pancakes, symbolise the miracle, because they are fried in oil.

Ingredients

(Use planet friendly, fairly traded, free-range ingredients wherever possible.)

Makes approximately 20

5 fat potatoes

1 large onion (optional)

3 medium eggs (beaten)

Nutmeg (optional)

1 tsp salt

half tsp pepper

Oil for frying

To serve: sour cream and apple sauce.

Method

Peel the potatoes and grate into a bowl of cold water. Leave to stand for 20 minutes, swirling occasionally, to extract cloudy potato starch. Drain off into a colander, pushing down with a spoon to squeeze out as much liquid as possible. Tip grated potato into a clean tea towel, wrap up and squeeze to extract any last drops of moisture.

Put potato into a bowl, grate in the onion if using, add salt and pepper and a grate of fresh nutmeg. Stir in beaten egg until evenly mixed. Heat 1cm of vegetable oil in a medium-sized frying pan until a shred of onion sizzles vigorously when dropped into it. Put dollops of potato mixture (about 2 to 3 tbsp) into the fat and gently squish down with the back of the ladle/spoon to make a pattie shape.

Turn down heat slightly and watch the latkes carefully. Turn them over when a golden fringe appears around the edges. Place a layer of kitchen paper under a cooling rack. When the latkes are golden on both sides, remove with a slotted spoon and place on the cooling rack. Serve while still quite hot with dollops of sour cream and apple sauce.

Jewish Food Blessings

Deuteronomy 8 in the Torah contains a commandment: 'And you shall eat and be satisfied, and you shall bless the Lord your G-d'. These words have led to the entire Jewish tradition of food *brachot* (blessings).

Blessings are an integral part of Jewish meals. There are different blessings for different food types before eating, and blessings for afterwards, when people have finished their meal. Here is an example of a *birkat hamazon* (grace after meals) which is said when eating in a group.

Leader: 'Let us praise G-d!'

Group: 'Praised be the name of G-d, now and forever.'

Leader: 'Praised be the name of G-d, now and forever. Praised be our G-d, of whose abundance we have eaten.'

Group: 'Praised be our G-d, of whose abundance we have eaten, and by whose goodness we live.'

Leader: 'Praised be our G-d, of whose abundance we have eaten, and by whose goodness we live. Praised be the Eternal G-d.'

All: 'Sovereign G-d of the universe, we praise You: Your goodness sustains the world. You are the G-d of grace, love, and compassion, the Source of bread for all who live; for Your love is everlasting. In Your great goodness we need never lack for food; You provide food enough for all. We praise You, O G-d, Source of food for all who live.'

something that unsettles our souls

"And the Lord G-d planted a garden eastward, in Eden"

– Genesis 2:8

Most people are asleep at the wheel when it comes to thinking about food, says Rabbi Noah Zvi Farkas. He serves at one of the biggest Conservative synagogues in the United States, Valley Beth Shalom in Encino, California, but he is also a co-founder of Netiya, a Jewish network that promotes urban agriculture, creating food gardens on unused institutional land in Los Angeles.

'Every person thinks about eating multiple times a day. Yet thinking about eating and thinking about food are different things,' he says. 'Most Americans have a vague idea where their food comes from, its ingredients, and whom it empowers or impoverishes along the way.'

Rabbi Noah describes this as 'epicurean narcolepsy' and says it is destroying our environment, making us sick and enslaving human beings to one another: 'We cannot understand our food if we do not understand how food empowers or impoverishes those who produce it and those who eat it.' So what can we do about it? The Rabbi says what we need is 'something that unsettles our souls' — and one way to begin this journey is by eating more spiritually.

'I remember once eating a fresh peach right off the tree. The yellow flesh, warm from the sun, melted in my mouth like a sun-kissed pudding. The second emotion I felt when eating that peach (the first was total bliss) was gratitude. Thanks for putting me in this place at this time to eat a wonderful fruit.

'In rabbinic tradition, the connection to food and to its depths through giving thanks is blessing. By reciting blessings, you bring the spiritual dimension into your food life and embed yourself in the natural world by connection to the Life Force that undergirds all of creation.'

Everyone has a Food Story

Every week Jewish food activist Karyn Moskowitz makes a 100-mile round trip to a produce market to buy organically grown fruit and vegetables.

She brings them to the Redeemer Lutheran Church in Louisville, Kentucky, where volunteers divide it up into baskets that parishioners can buy on a sliding scale of $12 to $25, with higher-income members subsidising their lower-income neighbours.

'When we showed up, the people freaked,' Karyn says. 'They said, "Where did you get that food? We can't buy anything like it here."'

Karyn runs New Roots, a not-for-profit organisation founded in 2009 that connects families to farms to provide fresh, affordable fruit and vegetables in parts of Louisville that do not have grocery stores or farmers' markets. It does so through four Fresh Stops, based at churches or schools, which to date, have linked up 800 families and 25 Kentucky farmers.

The Fresh Stops are largely run by volunteer leaders from the neighbourhood who sort the produce and divide it by the number of families that have bought ahead of time.

They label each box of produce with the amount each family should take that week — for example, ten tomatoes, five onions and two cabbages. The families then pay in advance for the next Fresh Stop.

Participants pool their money to purchase in bulk, but Karyn says this is not a charity project: 'It's not me saying to them, let me serve you. It's them calling me up and saying, I hear you know how to get food, let's work together.'

Studies show that low-income Louisvillians live 13 years less than their more affluent counterparts, partly due to lack of access to fresh food. 'Food apartheid' has existed in Louisville since at least the 1950s, says Karyn, but was not spoken about until New Roots began talking to local people about their food stories in 2011.

'So let me paint a picture of a Fresh Stop. Where else can you really go in West Louisville,' she asks, 'to see literally mountains of Technicolor local organic produce piled on church tables? Watch a nine-year-old football player eat his first plate of succotash [a dish of corn and lima beans] and ask for seconds, while his mother, who just informed us that her kids would not touch vegetables, looks on incredulously?

'I could tell you about all of the chefs who volunteered their time, or about Jennifer Hardy, mom of fifth grader Summer Gripps from the Wellington Fresh Stop, who stays up at night calling other moms to remind them to purchase their shares, and who told me recently that the Fresh Stops have

Taking the long-term view

Once, while the sage, Honi, was walking along a road, he saw an old man planting a carob tree. Honi asked him: 'How many years will it take for this tree to give forth its fruit?' The man answered that it would require 70 years. Honi asked: 'Are you so healthy a man that you expect to live that length of time and eat its fruit?' The man answered: 'I found a fruitful world because my ancestors planted it for me. So, too, will I plant for my children.'

– Babylonian Talmud, Ta'anit 23a

Wrap In Newspaper 2-3 days To Soften

Photo credit: New Roots

literally saved her life, put her diabetes in check, her weight down. Or our farmers, like farmer Larry Ayres whose Gala apples have set the taste buds of Louisville's food deserts on fire this summer.

there is a buzz going on in the room around food

'But really, the story that I would most like to tell are the stories of our Fresh Stop leaders, volunteers like Mary Montgomery who spend all their free time working together to create a food system that until recently, had just about completely bypassed them.

'These are the people that we hear people talk about so often, saying, "they just need to be educated" or "even if we put salads in our fast food restaurants, they only want to eat the fried high-calorie food".

'This issue is very complex, I will grant you that. But I have learned this: everyone has a food story to tell. People living in underinvested neighbourhoods, what we typically refer to as 'food deserts', are not waiting for us to "educate them". They know.

'They know that their food stories have been buried under lives of stress, often working two jobs to make ends meet, with no time for cooking from scratch.

'That our neighbourhoods are filled with cheap high-calorie meals, that isn't really food, but rather substances that are truly addictive and very hard to get away from once you start, especially soda. That we have been advertised to death, literally.

'This is why at New Roots we focus on creating community and reclaiming food sto-

ries. And when you walk in a Fresh Stop, you feel that. There is a buzz going on in the room around food. The food really glows, and creates that feeling inside you that you simply have to eat it because it is so beautiful, and indeed tastes real, not like the Styrofoam sitting in most of our grocery stores.

'When we know our farmers, and spend even just one season with them, we understand how hard it is for them to grow this food for us. And we have an incentive to eat it.

'When we pay $12 ahead of time, out of our food stamp budget, when we spend our volunteer hours calling farmers, collecting money, setting up tables, ordering pint containers, creating recipes and newsletters, and the list goes on, as most of our neighbourhood leaders do, we know we had better not waste our investment.

'What makes it a challenge is the only people against us are the processed food industry, the people who make drugs like statins, the people who make stents, and do bypasses and other doctors.

'The New Roots Fresh Stop Project is a people's movement, operating in the trenches in this modern-day battle for our lives and the lives of our future leaders.'

Reconnecting People to the Land where their Food is Grown

Every week during the summer months, thousands of Jewish families visit their local synagogue, community centre or school.

Not very surprising, you might think — except that this is to pick up a box of vegetables. They are part of a programme linking the American Jewish community with local farmers that results in nearly $5 million being invested in sustainable agriculture every year.

It is organised by the Jewish food and environment group Hazon and it is known as Community Supported Agriculture (CSA). The concept goes back to the 1980s in the US, inspired partly by radical new ideas from Europe about reconnecting people to the land where their food is grown. CSAs are a way for farmers to link up with buyers, and for buyers to make a more personal connection with how their food is grown.

Members pay up front for a 'share' which provides the farmer with some financial security and gives them fresh, healthy, local, mostly organic vegetables (and, in some cases, fruits, eggs, flowers and herbs) during the growing season.

Since Hazon's CSA programme launched in 2004 with one farm and a partnering synagogue, it has grown to include more than 65 sites and 2,300 households in the US, Canada and Israel. But as well as collecting their weekly greens, Hazon's CSA members also organise educational and social activities that 'connect the dots between Jewish tradition and agriculture', says American food writer Leah Koenig.

These often include at least one farm trip per season as well as potluck meals and sometimes cooking classes. One CSA held a retreat at its partner farm during Sukkot, a harvest festival commemorating the 40 years Jews spent wandering in the desert after their exodus from Egypt. As part of the festival, many Jewish families build temporary shelters or *sukkahs* (Sukkot means Feast of Booths) and the CSA members ate and slept in a sukkah they built together in the fields, simultaneously celebrating Sukkot and the harvesting taking place on the farm.

Another CSA brought a local chef to the congregation to prepare a CSA-to-table dinner, using only ingredients that were found in that week's box. As they ate their delicious dinner, members used texts from *Food for Thought*, Hazon's sourcebook on Jews, food and contemporary life, to discuss ideas about expanding the principle of kosher to include food that is 'fit' for the Earth.

Call to Action:
Worship and
Celebration

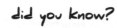

did you know?

Sikhism's holiest site, the Golden Temple in Amritsar, northern India, has pledged to provide organic, pesticide-free food and safe drinking water to the 30 million pilgrims visiting every year.

The 'Green Hospitality' project at the holy Armenian Orthodox shrine of Etchmiadzin provides traditional Armenian food for up to 100 visitors at a time, using local produce cooked on an environmentally friendly Armenian 'toner' fireplace by young people learning about their food heritage. Since joining the Green Pilgrimage Network they have used the '70-50-30' principle (see page 129) to ensure their food is as healthy and sustainable as possible.

Action Points

- Are the food, wine or flowers used in your worship the best they could be? A few years ago, Dr Rowan Williams, then Archbishop of Canterbury, said Anglicans should use organic bread and wine for Holy Communion. The Bhumi Project also recommends that Hindu temples opt for organic and locally grown fruit and flowers, saying: 'In making our offering to the Lord we want the best, to be as devotional as possible.'

- Does your faith community serve food or drinks after worship? Is it sustainably produced, fairly traded and locally sourced as much as possible?

- If not, why not form a committee to develop a food-sourcing policy — and make sure it is implemented.

- Does your faith group have a restaurant, café or retreat centre? Try to follow the Soil Association's recommendation that the food served should be 70% fresh, 50% locally produced and 30% organic. And ensure that animal-derived foods such as meat, milk and eggs are produced to as high welfare standards as you can manage.

Small changes can make big differences.

Commit to adopting one of these ideas in your faith practice.

- Celebrations play a big part in religious life. Christians have Easter, Muslims have Eid, Hindus have Diwali, Jews have Hanukkah, Buddhists have Vesak, Sikhs have Vaisakhi, to name but a few. There are also family occasions such as baptisms, weddings, bar/bat mitzvahs and funerals. Could you ensure the food served at these events is kinder to the Earth?

- Use your harvest celebration to promote real, sustainable food.

- Provide glasses and clean water at gatherings instead of plastic bottles of water.

- Look at the food connection around holy days of feasting or fasting; suggest a 'carbon fast' during Lent or Ramadan, for example.

- Celebrate your achievements — tell others what you are doing (and why) using websites, posters, social media, talks, sermons, photographs, engaging local press and digital media.

- Create new faith-based traditions — such as planting trees to celebrate a wedding or birth, or to commemorate a loved one's death.

Food and Worship in Islam

"The Earth is green and beautiful, and Allah has appointed you his stewards over it. The whole Earth has been created a place of worship, pure and clean."

– Hadith

Food is
What it is All About

"O ye people: Eat of what is lawful and good on earth"

— *Qur'an (Surah 2:168)*

I love food, I love to cook it, smell all the different aromas and try different recipes and I really get a kick out of serving food to people and having them enjoy their meal. If there is one thing that the Muslim communities around the world will agree upon, it is that food is what it is all about!

I am sure you will agree that the smells, flavours and taste of delicious food are wonderful triggers for lost memories, which can take you back to a time that holds precious moments. However, there are so many millions who are less fortunate than us, for whom a morsel of food is the difference between starvation and survival.

In Surah 7:31, the Qur'an says: 'Eat and drink but waste not by excess, for Allah loveth not the wasters.' In these times of austerity and the economic crisis facing the Western world there are lessons that can be learnt from the simplicity that is encountered in the faith communities. The Prophet (peace be upon him — PBUH) said: 'The child of Adam has not filled any receptacle worse than his stomach. It is sufficient for the child of Adam to eat small bits of food that keep him healthy. Now if he wants to eat much any way, he should give a third to the food, a third to the drink and a third (of his stomach) to let him breathe comfortably' (Ahmad).

In Islam the concept of food has both a spiritual, family and community element to it. In this hadith, by Sahih Muslim, 'The Prophet ordered us not to leave anything in the plate and he said: "You do not know in which portion of your food Allah has put the *barakah* [blessing]".'

This saying of the Prophet Muhammad (PBUH) shows that food is a blessing from Allah and therefore we should pay due attention to how we procure, prepare and consume food. *Halal* is an Arabic word,

For that We pour forth water in abundance,
And We split the earth in fragments,
And produce therein corn,
And grapes and nutritious plants,
And olives and dates,
And enclosed gardens, dense with lofty trees,
And fruits and fodder —
For use and convenience to you and your cattle.

— *Qur'an, 80:25–32*

Photo credit: Preston Rhea

which means 'permissible' and, used in the context of food, usually refers to what is permitted according to Islamic law.

Haram has the opposite meaning, that is, what is forbidden. So forbidden items include pork and all its products, animals improperly slaughtered, alcoholic drinks, carnivorous animals, birds of prey, and any food contaminated with any of these.

After ensuring that the food we are consuming is halal there are habits that Muslims incorporate into their lives as second nature which relate to food because the Qur'an and Sunnah have given us directions to follow in every aspect of our lives. Every day I remind my younger children of the proper Islamic etiquette that one should observe when eating, so that it is ingrained in them as they get older. This includes the following:

❧ Washing the hands before and after eating.

❧ Supplicating to Allah to bless the food.

❧ Saying 'Bismillah' (in the Name of Allah) before eating.

❧ Eating with the right hand.

❧ Eating from what is nearest on the plate to the person.

❧ Not criticising the food; if you like it, you should eat it, otherwise you should leave it.

❧ Eating with three fingers and not eating while leaning on something.

❧ Saying 'Alhamdulillah' (praise be to Allah) after finishing eating.

In today's materialistic world, it seems we have fewer opportunities to spend quality time with our families and loved ones. Technology has overtaken us, our lives have become too fast with little time for reflection and inner searching and peace. Instant gratification and greater demand for material items has made us lose a part of our humanity. Islam encourages a balanced approach to everything we do and encourages eating together in groups either as a family or with friends.

It is confirmed in the Sunnah, by Abu Dawood, that it is desirable to eat in a group and this is better than eating separately. It is reported that the companions asked the Prophet: 'O Prophet of Allah, we eat but we never eat our fill.' He said: 'It might be that you are eating separately.' They replied: 'Yes.' Thereupon, the Prophet said: 'Get together when you eat, and mention the Name of Allah (when you start eating), Allah will bless your food.'

Our religious traditions have a great deal to offer the world in the 21st century if we take the time to reflect upon them. We can bring balance to our spiritual, physical and social lives by reminding us to share our blessings and act responsibly.

Dr Husna Ahmad OBE is chief executive officer of Global One 2015, an international development organisation, and she also heads the UK-based environmental consultancy Green Pearl Consulting.

Islamic scriptures

The Qur'an is Islam's holiest scripture and is believed to be the final revelation of God. Muslims are also guided by the Sunnah (the way the Prophet Muhammad lived his life), and the Hadith (reports of the Prophet's actions and sayings by his companions).

To be accepted as true, each report has to be traceable through an unbroken series of reliable authorities, with the name of the original authority or the final collector being the one given to it to this day. For example, a hadith attributed to 'Muslim' comes from Sahih Muslim, a collection compiled by Imam Muslim ibn al-Hajjaj al-Naysaburi, considered to be one of the most authoritative.

Muslims generally use the salutation 'Peace be upon Him' whenever they mention the Prophet Muhammad's name as a mark of respect. This is usually abbreviated to PBUH in text and stems from the instruction in the Qur'an (al-Ahzab 33:56): 'Lo! Allah and His angels shower blessings on the Prophet. O ye who believe! Ask blessings on him and salute him with a worthy salutation.' However, PBUH is not used in quotations from scripture.

There's a Buzz about Kingston Mosque...

British mosques have swelled their congregations by tens of thousands — with the successful introduction of bees to their premises.

Kingston Mosque in Surrey, Britain, is celebrating its third year of keeping a bee-hive on its roof, close to the minaret.

News of dwindling bee numbers and the medicinal properties of honey prompted committee member Munir Ravalia, to persuade London's East Road Mosque to set up a hive. Munir said: 'Once we dealt with worries about safety, lots of people were just curious about how it would all work and when they would be able to get some honey!'

The Kingston Mosque initiative was the model for East London Mosque introducing some 40,000 new bees to its roof in 2011 through local bee-keeper Khalil Attan.

Great Idea!

'We Can't Just Close Our Eyes'

As the baking Sudanese sun beat down on Lutfi Radwan's head while he spent his days inspecting farms, he dreamed of the cool, green English countryside at home where he could grow his own crops and rear contented animals.

He and his wife Ruby wanted to combine their religious values and love of nature to create a sustainable, environmentally friendly business that would also be a way of life for them and their children.

Ten years later in 2002 the couple bought 45 acres in Hampton Gay, Oxfordshire, and set about creating Britain's first organic halal farm. Today, Willowbrook Organic Farm produces naturally and organically reared chicken, lamb and eggs. The farm is also partially powered by wind energy and electricity generated by solar panels.

Lutfi and Ruby's three eldest children Asiyla, Adam and Khalil help run the business while the two younger ones, Ali, pictured with the pygmy goats, and Camilla, help out with the fun jobs, such as feeding newborn lambs and looking after Gracie the pony.

Khalil says the help they receive from volunteers with Worldwide Opportunities on Organic Farms (WWOOF) is invaluable. 'We are learning everything as we go along, starting everything from scratch — even the website — with help from family and friends. 'We couldn't do everything around the farm without the help of the WWOOF volunteers.'

Animal welfare is top of the agenda for the Radwans, which is one of the reasons why they wanted to farm in the first place. Lutfi says: 'We felt neither the welfare side of taking care of animals or the ritual side of mentioning God's name was observed very well in the modern food industry.

'We've established Willowbrook on what we believe are Islamic principles, which are very close to the ideas of organic, sustainable and environmentally sound practices. The Prophet Muhammad forbade eating food when the animal was abused. If that's the case, we have to look at what's happening around us. We can't just close our eyes.'

Lutfi is appalled by the conditions in which billions of chickens are raised for the table all over the world. He says: 'It's really like a concentration camp. Chickens can be crammed into dense conditions where there's a lot of suffering or they are simply thrown away as so many are bred.'

'But the end product — the customer is distanced from it. They don't see it until it's wrapped in a plastic bag and handed to them.'

The Radwans' farm practices and attention to detail mean their customers can enjoy top-quality meat while being confident that the animals have been reared in the kindest way possible and that the land is being looked after.

One of their customers says: 'It is so good being able to buy from real people you can actually meet, talk to, and trust. High animal welfare standards are very important to me and I know Ruby and Lutfi provide the best possible care for all their livestock. I like to support organic farming whenever I can; it is so important to keep our soil in good order so that it will stay productive for those who follow after us.'

Other activities at the farm include workshop weekends, open days, concerts, school visits and it also offers camping facilities. In June 2014 Willowbrook was the finishing post for the first Tour de Farm, organised by MADE In Europe, a Muslim-led movement of young people campaigning against global poverty and injustice. The 100-kilometre Tour de Farm started in London and finished with an ethical barbecue.

Photo credit: Ruby Radwan, Willowbrook Organic Farm

Islamic Farming

In the first weeks of 2014, a very special workshop was held in Nairobi, Kenya. Around 30 imams had gathered in Nairobi from all over Kenya to learn the practical techniques involved in farming sustainably — one that is based on Islamic teachings about caring for Allah's creation.

This was the first training workshop in a new faith-based approach to agriculture entitled Islamic Farming, developed by the Alliance of Religions and Conservation (ARC) and UK-based international Muslim NGO Global One 2015 following requests from ARC's Muslim faith partners.

The seeds of this new approach go back to ARC's Nairobi celebration in 2012 to launch 27 long-term plans on the environment developed by Christian, Muslim and Hindu faith groups in sub-Saharan Africa.

During the two-day meeting, Muslim participants listened with great interest to the presentations on Farming God's Way (see story on page 18).

They were particularly struck by the way this Christian approach to farming both improved crop yields and protected the environment through linking a farmer's faith beliefs to the way she or he cared for the land. At the end they had a question: 'What

about Muslim farmers? Why isn't there a faith-based approach to farming for us?'

It was a good question; out of 910 million people in sub-Saharan Africa, 248 million are Muslim, and many are small-scale farmers. As a result of this call, ARC and Global One 2015 began working with Muslim faith partners in Africa to develop a faith-based manual and training programme inspired by Islamic teachings and beliefs.

This would be the first manual specially designed for Muslim farmers using the practical principles of conservation agriculture (a way of farming promoted by the UN's Food and Agriculture Organization as being both environmentally sustainable and climate smart) but with a spiritual foundation that

> And it is He Who produces gardens with trellises and without, and dates, and tilth with produce of all kinds, and olives and pomegranates
>
> – Qur'an, 6:141

Photo credit: ARC

is entirely based upon Islamic scriptures and teachings.

The first step was a thorough theological assessment of Islamic scriptures. Focus group meetings were held with Muslim clerics and scholars in Kampala and Nairobi to consider issues around Islam and farming and there was tremendous enthusiasm for the project from all involved.

In Uganda, a number of Muslim farmers attended a Christian Farming God's Way workshop so that they could see how the Christian faith was integral to the teaching, while also learning the practical techniques used. All were impressed by what they learned.

The results, which came after a prolonged dry period in which conventional crops experienced almost total crop failure, amazed her. Even though she had started her planting late with little time to prepare her land properly, her Farming God's Way plot had a 50% survival rate, showing it dealt with the very dry conditions much better than the conventional plots. And her Farming God's Way maize cobs were twice the size of the traditionally farmed maize: 'This Farming God's Way really works!' said Hajjat, pictured overleaf in the foreground, smiling broadly.

Delighted though she was, Hajjat's success brought its own unexpected problems: 'Many people resorted to stealing from our Farming God's Way plot as the cobs were really big, healthy and attractive,' she said, before shrugging philosophically. 'I understand why — they needed food.'

The *Islamic Farming* handbook was launched in Nairobi in March 2014 to great enthusiasm from the Muslim community. What makes Islamic Farming different is that it speaks to Muslim farmers in the language of the Qur'an and the Sunnah.

By integrating Islamic scriptures with practical teaching in conservation agriculture, the manual helps farmers grow food while also protecting the environment in a way that makes sense to them as Muslims.

The Supreme Council of Kenya Muslims, which represents Muslims in Kenya, has established a demonstration and training farm on a 700-acre site in Thika, Kenya. Another ten demonstration farms have been established elsewhere in Kenya and a further ten in Uganda.

Islamic Dietary Laws

"O ye who believe! Fasting is prescribed for you... that ye may (learn) self-restraint"

– Qur'an 2:183

There are 1.34 billion Muslims globally, 20% of the world's population. Islam is the state religion of 25 countries. For all Muslims, what they eat, how they eat and regular periods of fasting all form a core part of faith practice. Muslims are told to eat what is lawful (permitted) and 'good' (pure, clean and wholesome). Islamic dietary rules are contained in the Qur'an, the Sunnah and Hadith.

They define foods that are *halal* (lawful or permitted), and *haram* (unlawful or forbidden). Haram foods include pork or pork-based products, meat from animals not slaughtered in the prescribed Islamic way or already dead before slaughter, as well as any food or drink containing alcohol or other intoxicants. Other haram foods are blood and blood by-products, carnivorous animals and birds of prey and some non-halal additives such as food colouring E120, a red dye made from cochineal insects, and E542, an anti-caking agent made from animal bones. Halal foods include milk (from cows, sheep, camels, and goats), honey, fish, vegetables and fruits, legumes and nuts such as peanuts, cashew nuts and walnuts, and grains such as wheat, rice, rye, barley and oats.

Muslims are also required to recite the name of God over the food before eating and to fast regularly. The main fasting period is Ramadan, the ninth month of the Muslim calendar, when abstaining from food or drink from dawn to sunset is mandatory for all healthy adults, with a few exceptions such as of those who are travelling or pregnant women. The aim is to help teach self-discipline, self-restraint and empathy with the suffering of the poor.

During Ramadan, which runs for approximately 30 days, Muslims begin their days with *suhoor*, a meal taken just before sunrise, and end with *iftar*, eaten after sunset. The end of Ramadan is marked by Eid-ul-Fitr — the Festival of the Breaking of the Fast. It's a time of joy, forgiveness and making amends.

Islamic food prayers

Muslims pray before and after every meal. This is not a communal grace, and nor is it part of the ritual prayers that Muslims are required to carry out five times a day, called **Salat** (the practice of formal worship considered one of the five pillars, or foundations, of Islam), but rather a silent individual prayer to acknowledge that all blessings come from Allah.

Before eating: 'With Allah's name and upon the blessings granted by Allah (do we eat).'

After eating: 'Praise be to Allah Who has fed us and given us drink, and made us Muslims.'

Islamic Festival Food

Eid al-Adha: Eid al-Adha, the Festival of the Sacrifice, celebrates how Ibrahim's devotion to Allah passed the sternest test. Allah appeared to Ibrahim in a dream and asked him to sacrifice his son, Ishmael, to prove his faith.

Ibrahim was on the verge of killing his son when Allah appeared and gave him a lamb to kill instead. Today, lamb is on the menu at this special time of year to remind Muslims of Ibrahim's willingness to sacrifice his own son for Allah.

Lamb Biryani

Ingredients

(Use planet friendly, fairly traded, free-range ingredients wherever possible.)

Serves 4

For the marinade:

450g / 1 lb lamb, diced into bite-size pieces

2cm ginger, peeled and grated

3 cloves garlic, crushed

1 tsp chilli powder

1 tsp salt

1 tsp turmeric

3 tsp garam masala

2 tsp ground coriander

2 tsp ground cumin

1 tsp black peppercorns, crushed

1 stick cinnamon, broken in half

2 tbsp sunflower oil

1 tsp cumin seeds

To cook the dish:

300g / 11 oz / 1 cup
basmati rice

500ml / 17 fl oz
vegetable stock

3 tomatoes,
remove seeds and dice

2 onions, sliced

Large handful spinach

3 bay leaves

125ml / 4fl oz
natural yogurt to serve

Method

Place all ingredients for the marinade in a glass bowl, mix well and chill for at least two hours — the longer the better. Remove from fridge one hour before cooking. Prepare the rice by soaking for at least 30 minutes and rinse in a sieve until the water runs clear.

Add the oil to a large, hot pan and fry the cumin seeds until they sizzle. Add the onion and fry until soft and brown. Pour in the lamb mix, add the tomatoes and continue to cook on a high heat for five minutes continually stirring to ensure the spices are thoroughly cooked. Turn the heat to low, cover and simmer for 25 minutes.

Add the bay leaves, rice and vegetable stock, stir and cover again. Leave on a low heat for a further 20 minutes. Turn off the heat, add spinach, stir once and replace the lid. Let this stand for ten minutes to ensure the rice is fluffy. Serve with natural yogurt.

Millet (funde) and Groundnut Soup

This recipe from Sierra Leone is prepared for Muslim festivals and feasts.

It comes from **Food for Life: Recipes and Stories on the Right to Food**, compiled by the Lutheran World Federation.

Ingredients

(Use planet friendly, fairly traded, free-range ingredients wherever possible.)

Serves 5

Ingredients for the funde:

4 cups millet
(one cup is 240ml
for this recipe)

1.5 litres / 50 fl oz
/ 6 and a half cups water

Method

Place the water in a saucepan and bring to the boil. Remove and keep aside some of the boiled water. Add millet to the saucepan and mix, add salt to taste and cook over a low heat for 10 to 15 minutes. Check if it is soft. If not, stir in some of the reserved hot water and allow it to steam until it is as soft as possible. Allow the mixture to dry.

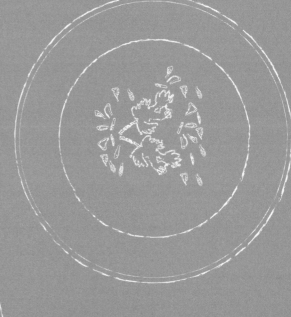

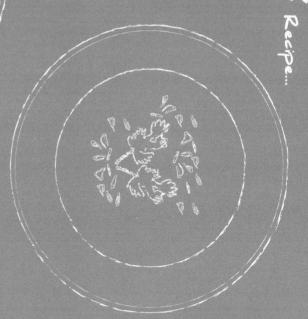

Ingredients for the groundnut soup:

500g / 1 lb 2oz
mutton or beef

1 aubergine (eggplant)

1 chopped tomato (optional)

150ml / 5oz / two thirds cup
groundnut paste

240ml / 8oz / 1 cup
chopped onion

1 bouillon cube

Salt and pepper to taste

360ml / 12 fl oz
/ 1 and a half cups water

Method

Place the meat, bouillon cube and water in a pan, bring to the boil and cook until the meat is tender. Peel the aubergine and slice into eight lengthwise. Rub the seeds with a knife to remove as many as possible. Cut into small cubes, wash and add to the meat. Boil until soft.

Add the groundnut paste and cook until any lumps have dissolved. Add salt and pepper to taste, and the onion. Add the tomato if using. Stir frequently and check the seasoning to taste.

Simmer until you are happy with the consistency and flavour. Remove from the heat and cool. Serve with the millet.

'As Women We Were Helpless before this Project'

Women produce most of the food grown by smallholder farmers in Africa yet they face an uphill struggle. Traditional inheritance laws mean land often goes to male relatives. Women also tend to have less access to money or resources, and often have less time to work their plots due to their other family responsibilities. In Gomba District, Uganda, a faith-based initiative seeks to change that.

Hadijah Namuli Semwanga and her husband Hamdan Semwanga have always grown cassava on their farm in Gomba, Uganda. But it is only in the past two years that they have grown enough to sell to the traders who travel two to three hours from the city of Kampala to buy this staple of Ugandan cuisine.

The profit they made from their cassava last year was enough to buy a second-hand motorbike and a young calf. Its dung is spread on their fields, nourishing the soil further, and soon they will begin harvesting their passion fruits, one of the new crops they have been encouraged to grow in between the rows of potato in their fields and supported by the newly planted Ficus trees.

These are some of the real benefits that have come to Hadijah and her husband following her participation in the Gomba Women's Environment Project. She is one of 32 women from five mosques in Gomba taking part in the initiative, which began in 2011 and aims to reduce the number of trees cut for firewood by planting at least 12,000 new trees every year and developing environmentally friendly income-generating activities. Fellow project member Nambi Aliziki says: 'The project started with tree planting and every member has to plant 300 trees. We also do poultry keeping and rear animals. Some have goats, some have cows. We also have stoves which use only a little firewood, and water tanks for harvesting water.'

Farmer Margret Setumba is thrilled. The money she earns by selling the fruit and vegetables she has grown helps to pay her children's school fees — and those of her orphaned grandchildren. Madina Tebasoka is also educating her children thanks to her new income earned from small-scale farming. She speaks for many when she says: 'As women we were helpless before this project.'

Project director Hajjat Aphwa Kaawaase Sebyala said people did not realise they were damaging the environment when they cut down all the trees before planting their crops. 'Our people are not sensitised to environmental issues. They have cut down all the trees in Gomba and our hills are bare, the rains are not coming and we have prolonged drought. They are not aware of the use of trees in preserving the environment,' she says. 'We advise them to leave the trees and plant the beans or maize or coffee under the trees. Now all our people are asking for seedlings because they are aware that the environment is very important, and those who have cut trees are replacing them. In the next few years we should see a better and greener Gomba.'

As well as indigenous species used for fuelwood, fodder and construction or to create windbreaks, many of the trees planted are fruit trees, such as paw paws, mangoes, guava and avocado. Tree planting, especially fruit trees, has special significance for Gomba's members because the Prophet Muhammad attached great importance to this activity.

Planting trees is also *Sadaqah Jariyah* (everlasting gift to Allah), a form of charity that provides everlasting rewards for as long as people benefit from your good deeds. In other words, a person who plants trees will keep on accumulating rewards even after death. And not just for planting the tree: he or she will be rewarded in this life and in the next if any human or animal eats the tree's produce.

Photo credit: ARC

Whoever plants a tree, reward will be recorded for him so long as it produces fruit.

– *Majma' al-Zawaid, v. 480*

One project member has established a tree nursery, selling avocado and jackfruit tree seedlings to other members at a reasonable price and earning money for herself at the same time, as well as planting them on her own land. 'In two or three years she'll get the fruits from these trees,' says Hajjat. 'She'll also be answering Sadaqah Jariyah.'

In fact, the project was so successful the women grew so much they were able to sell their produce and earn much-needed income for their families. Soon the men were volunteering to water their wives' plots for them to ensure the vegetables were well cared for.

This project succeeded because a ready source of water was available in the form of a dam built by Action Aid — another project in a different area failed for lack of water.

I Drink Tap!

Great Idea!

Sales of bottled water have doubled to 54 billion litres in Europe alone in the past ten years. And that's bad for the planet, says MADE in Europe, a Muslim-led movement of young people fighting global poverty and injustice.

So why is it so bad? Well, for every gallon of water that goes into plastic bottles, two gallons of water are wasted during production, says MADE. Other problems include multinationals buying public water supplies, leaving famers without enough water to grow their crops, and a system in which only one in five plastic bottles is recycled: the rest end up littering the environment, harming wildlife, or dumped in countries like India and China.

'Sadly, some Muslim community institutions are among the worst culprits when it comes to promoting bottled water, from our mosques which give out thousands of bottles during *iftar* and *tarawih*, to our charities who use the bottles to advertise themselves,' says MADE.

That's why it launched the I Drink Tap! Campaign calling on Muslims to reject plastic water bottles and urging mosques to install self-service water coolers connected to mains water: 'They are not only environmentally friendly (no transportation costs, no plastic, no waste) but also very cost effective.'

Call to Action:
Buying

Case Study

For five days in May 2012, nearly 50 supporters of the Muslim Agency for Development Eduation (MADE) in Europe took up the challenge to Live Below the Line, spending only £1 per day for five days on food and drink. Volunteers experienced a brief taste of the hunger suffered by more than a billion people around the world. Nadeem Javaid, 27, said when he first heard about the challenge he thought it would be impossible but decided: 'We're Muslims, we fast, right? If I can do a month of Ramadan, surely I could manage Live Below the Line.

'In fact it was harder as there was no massive feast waiting for me at the end of the day. I lived on 20p porridge with water, and enough daal and chickpeas to last me a lifetime! Live Below the Line proved to be a profoundly spiritual journey.

'For the first time in my life I was connecting with the food I ate, becoming more conscious of my spending habits and truly being thankful to Allah for what He has provided for me.'

Small changes can make big differences.

Commit to adopting one of these ideas in your daily life.

Action Points

- Buy seasonal fruit and vegetables — they're more climate-friendly as well as freshest and tastiest.

- Eat locally produced food where possible — it reduces food miles and keeps money in the community.

- Try to buy directly from producers if you can — shop at farmers' markets and farm shops, or consider getting a 'veg box' delivery.

- Look for certification of organic produce, Fairtrade or MSC (Marine Stewardship Council) for sustainably caught fish. Support retailers that stock these or similarly labelled products.

- Think about food miles — how far has it been carried already? Challenge yourself to achieve the '100-mile diet' (80% of your food comes from within 100 miles from your home).

- When thinking of food miles, don't forget the ones you create. Walk or cycle to the shops instead of driving.

- Try to avoid anything with more than five ingredients — additives are rarely good for you.

- Plan your menus and shop accordingly rather than grabbing stuff you might not use in the end.

- If you feel your local supermarket should stock more sustainable produce, ask to see the manager and discuss it.

- Ask restaurants and suppliers about their sourcing. If enough people ask about organic meat or free-range eggs, then suppliers will stock it.

Faith, Food and Farm Animals

"The greatness of a nation and its moral progress can be judged by the way its animals are treated."

– *Mahatma Gandhi*
Indian spiritual and political leader, 1869–1948

The Misery of Intensive Farming

"Industrial agriculture is one of the top four things for which future generations will condemn us"

— Kwame Anthony Appiah, Philosophy Professor at Princeton University

What does a farm look like? A combination of clever marketing campaigns and misty-eyed nostalgia has many people imagining farms as something out of the Old MacDonald nursery rhyme of childhood, with chickens clucking contentedly in a yard and cows, pigs and sheep grazing in nearby grassy fields. And even though many of us know that the reality is a little different, most of us have no idea of the extent of the difference.

Today, most farm animals in Europe and North America (and increasingly in the rest of the world too) are reared intensively. And that means that animals have little or no access to the outdoors at all.

Take chickens. In 1950, chicken was such a treat that most British people ate less than a kilo a year. Now we eat more than 30 times that amount (around 31kg per year), according to Compassion in World Farming. In 2011 the UK slaughtered around 850 million hens for meat, yet how many of us are aware of chickens as we drive through the countryside? We rarely see one and that's because most chickens spend their short lives crammed into giant sheds housing tens of thousands of hens.

Factory farms, which in America the industry prefers to call CAFOs — 'concentrated animal feeding operations' — are the fastest growing system of meat production worldwide, according to the UN Food and Agriculture Organization. It says global meat production has quadrupled since the early 1960s and two out of every three farm animals in the world are now factory farmed. Factory farming now accounts for around three-quarters of poultry production, two-thirds of egg production, and more than half of pork production.

compassionate, kind and decent?

It is only through this kind of intensive operation that meat can be supplied as cheaply and in the abundance that we demand. But at what price? What does this intensive production mean for the welfare of farm animals, the environment and even ourselves? If we were faced with the reality of these factory farms, would we see them as compassionate, kind and decent?

Would we show them to our children? Or would we hide from them the realities of the farrowing pens in which intensively farmed

sows are held, unable to turn as they give birth? The baby chicks, injured or sick or simply male, discarded by hand or conveyor belt and gassed to death or tossed alive into giant electronic mincers in what the industry terms 'instantaneous mechanical destruction'?

Factory farming may be an 'efficient' way of producing large amounts of meat but it also creates high levels of waste, uses huge amounts of water and land to produce feed, contributes to the spread of human and animal diseases, and plays a role in biodiversity loss, according to the US-based research organisation, the Worldwatch Institute.

Farm animal production contributes to climate change: the industry accounts for an estimated 18% of the world's greenhouse gas emissions, including 9% of carbon dioxide emissions, nearly 40% of methane

(a greenhouse gas 25 times more potent than carbon dioxide), and 65% of nitrous oxide (300 times more potent than carbon dioxide). Suppressing infection among livestock reared in intensive operations often means using large amounts of antibiotics, thus greatly increasing the risk of antibiotic resistance, and that has huge implications for human health. Despite this, approximately 75% of the new diseases that affected humans from 1999 to 2009 originated in animals or animal products.

In the next few pages, Joyce D'Silva, ambassador for leading farm animal welfare charity Compassion in World Farming, looks at conditions of factory farm animals, which until 2009 were not, in Europe, defined as sentient beings. And Sue Dibb examines what we need to do if we are to reverse the trend for greater intensification of the livestock industry.

Fluffy Chick to Chicken Dinner in just Six Weeks

"Being kind to animals, saving them, and protecting them is not a matter of religion... It is something everyone should do"

– The 14th Dalai Lama Tenzin Gyatso

Although the major faiths view animals as creatures of God or as sentient beings with which we share the Earth, there is no universal teaching on how we should relate to them. Farm animals — the ones we eat — are perhaps the most neglected. Yet we know that they too are individual creatures, capable of pain and suffering or pleasure and probably joy as well.

Compassion in World Farming was founded in 1967 by a British farmer who became horrified by the development of modern, intensive factory farming. Peter Roberts, a deeply spiritual man, was once asked to define 'factory farming'. His response: 'Factory farming begins where the individuality of the animal ends.'

I invite you to look into the factory farm. See the 20,000 chickens being reared for meat, crammed into a barren shed, bred for unnatural, super-fast growth, more than a quarter of them suffering from lameness as their skeletons can no longer bear the weight of their fast-growing bodies. Fluffy chick to chicken dinner in just six weeks.

Look into the typical pig farm. See the young pigs being fattened for our plates, jostling each other for space in their dark and crowded pens, slipping on the uncomfortable slatted floor, desperate to sink their highly sensitive snouts into soil they will never get to see. See the breeding sows, in some countries still confined and unable to turn round throughout their four-month pregnancies and still usually imprisoned in narrow farrowing crates while giving birth and suckling their piglets. See the caged egg-laying hens, standing day after day on the wire mesh floor, unable to nest properly to lay their eggs, unable to stretch their wings or fly up to roost at night.

See the massive turkey farm, the creatures often grown to celebrate the Christian festival of Christmas. These birds have been bred to grow so large that the breeding turkeys are unable to mate naturally, as the weight of the male would damage the female, so breeding is done by artificial insemination.

See the anguish of the dairy cow, her calf removed just one day after birth, bred to produce about ten times the amount of milk that her calf would have drunk from her (but never does). See the new mega-dairy farms, where the cow herself will never get to graze on green pasture, but has to endure a shortened life on concrete and sand.

In the United States, just four companies produce 81% of the cows, 73% of the sheep, 50% of the chickens, and 60% of the pigs that Americans eat, according to the Animal Legal & Historical Center.

We slaughter globally more than 60 billion animals for food each year, a figure set to roughly double in the next half-century as Western dietary habits spread to the growing urban middle classes around the world. Already two-thirds of farm animals are kept like this, denied any quality of life, any joy in their own existence. Even the animals' last days and weeks are often sullied by terrifying journeys to distant slaughterhouses. See the millions of animals transported by ship or truck every year, often in foul conditions, from country to country, continent to continent, just to be slaughtered on arrival. Australia to the Middle East, South America to Turkey, Ireland to Libya, Poland to Italy — the list is endless.

In the quest to speed up so-called 'breed improvements', farm animals are already being cloned and genetically engineered, often causing great suffering to the resulting offspring. Within months or a few years meat and milk from these animals may be on our dinner tables — another product of misery. Yet science is now constantly uncovering more capacities of animals — to anticipate, to make conscious choices, to use tools, to communicate with sound, to express empathy.

Holy books, often dating from many hundreds of years ago, were not written in a context of factory farming, cloning and genetic engineering of farm animals. But they can perhaps elucidate some basic principles to guide us. The Qur'an tells us that 'All the creatures on earth, and all the birds that fly with wings, are communities like you.'

Some Buddhist texts recognise that animals have the capacity to have feelings and exhort us to be compassionate towards them: 'All beings seek for happiness; so let your compassion extend itself to all.' (Mahavamsa).

One of the ancient holy books of the Hindu tradition, the Shvetashvatara Upanishad, says:

'As the sun shines and
fills all space with light,
Above, below, across,
so shines the Lord
Of Love and fills the
hearts of all created beings.'

The Bible implies that we should care for our farm animals: 'A righteous man regardeth the life of his beast.' How should we respond with the insights provided by faith teachings and the knowledge we gain from science? Can we be free of our family or cultural conditioning and just 'look the animals in the eye' and respond in the light of our own conscience?

Can we reduce our consumption of animal products? Can we choose meat, eggs and milk from animals which have lived on free-range or organic farms? Can we work, each in our own way, to make things better?

Photo credit: Compassion in World Farming

Joyce D'Silva is ambassador for Compassion in World Farming, the leading farm animal welfare charity that campaigns to end the factory farming of animals and long-distance transport.

Farmageddon: The True Cost of Cheap Meat by CIWF chief executive Philip Lymbery, with Isabel Oakeshott, is published by Bloomsbury. The book examines the impact of the intensive livestock industry which has seen farm animals disappear from our fields as the production of food has become a global industry. Lymbery and Oakeshott argue that we are reaching a tipping point as the farming revolution threatens our countryside, health and the quality of our food wherever we live in the world.

Good Egg Award

Since 2007, Compassion in World Farming's Good Egg Award has celebrated food manufacturers and restaurateurs that use or have committed to use cage-free eggs or egg products, benefiting more than 30 million laying hens each year.

It takes more than six billion laying hens to supply the global egg market, and more than 60% of these hens are kept in industrialised caged systems, according to CIWF. Barren battery cages were banned in the European Union in 2012, marking a huge victory for animal welfare, although not all member states are fully compliant yet.

The barren battery cages crammed four or five hens together on wire mesh floors and with barely enough room for them to stand. By law, each hen was entitled to no more floor space than an A4 sheet of paper. Stacked in rows several tiers high, often in closed sheds housing thousands of birds, hens led lives of misery in these cruel conditions.

Since the ban, the industry has introduced 'enriched cages' which are bigger and designed to give hens more freedoms, including opportunities to perch or roost. They are a step forward, but still not good enough, say campaigners. And in many other parts of the world, the battery cages are widely used. In the USA, for example, nearly all laying hens are in barren battery cages, says CIWF.

a life free from fear and distress

In the 1960s, the massive growth in intensive animal husbandry that had taken place over the previous few decades prompted the UK government to look at the welfare of animals reared in factory-farming conditions. The resulting Brambell Report, published in 1965, set for the first time basic standards for farm animals — specifically that they should have freedom 'to stand up, lie down, turn around, groom themselves and stretch their limbs'.

Since then, the 'five freedoms' have developed to include the idea that the welfare of an animal includes its physical and mental state. Britain's Farm Animal Welfare Committee considers that good animal welfare implies both fitness and a sense of wellbeing. Any animal kept by humans must, at least, be protected from unnecessary suffering. It believes an animal's welfare, whether on farm, in transit, at market or at a place of slaughter, should be considered in terms of the following 'five freedoms'.

❧ Freedom from hunger and thirst: by ready access to fresh water and a diet to maintain full health and vigour.

❧ Freedom from discomfort: by providing an appropriate environment including shelter and a comfortable resting area.

❧ Freedom from pain, injury or disease: by prevention or rapid diagnosis and treatment.

❧ Freedom to express normal behaviour: by providing sufficient space, proper facilities and company of the animal's own kind.

❧ Freedom from fear and distress: by ensuring conditions and treatment that avoid mental suffering.

what are feedlots?

In the United States, cattle are often kept in barren, grass-less, crowded pens known as feedlots to be fattened up for several months before slaughter by being fed on grain — which cows' stomachs are not designed to digest efficiently. These feedlots can be enormous, containing 20,000 or more cows, and often bordered by lagoons of animal waste created from their urine and faeces.

To give an idea of their size, figures compiled in 2013 by the Kansas Department of Agriculture Division of Animal Health showed there were at least 12 feedlots in Finney County, south-west Kansas, containing more than 305,000 head of cattle. The county has a human population of just 37,000.

Princeton University professor of philosophy Kwame Anthony Appiah says: 'Of the more than 90 million cattle in our country, at least 10 million at any time are packed into feedlots, saved from the inevitable diseases of overcrowding only by regular doses of antibiotics, surrounded by piles of their own faeces, their nostrils filled with the smell of their own urine. Picture it — and then imagine your grandchildren seeing that picture.'

Inspiring Story from Islam

This story from Islam illustrating the Prophet's compassion for animals is told by one of his companions, Abu Huraira.

Because the animal in this case is a dog, it is even more striking, as many Muslims consider dogs to be unclean.

Abu Huraira, whose given name was Abd al-Rahman ibn Sakhr Al-Azdi, was also known for his kindness to animals: his name means 'father of kittens' because, one story goes, he used to carry kittens in the draped sleeves of his robe.

The Prophet said, 'While a man was walking he felt thirsty and went down a well and drank water from it. On coming out of it, he saw a dog panting and eating mud because it was so thirsty.

'He said to himself, "This dog is suffering from thirst as I was." So, he went down the well again and filled his shoe with water and gave it water.

'Allah thanked him for that deed and forgave him. The people said, "O Allah's Apostle! Is there a reward for us in serving the animals?" He replied: "Yes, there is a reward for serving any animate (living) being".'

Making Sense
of Labels

There are a growing number of labelling schemes on the market focusing on environmental sustainability and social justice. Picking your way through them can be confusing, especially when supermarkets and food companies label their products with meaningless phrases such as 'natural' and 'farm fresh' which are nothing more than a marketing ploy, says Compassion in World Farming.

Some of the main international labels include Fairtrade, which certifies that a product has met minimum social, economic and environmental standards; Rainforest Alliance, which works to biodiversity and ensure sustainable livelihoods; and Marine Stewardship Council, which certifies fish from wild-capture fisheries but not farmed fish.

Other marks include Leaf, for farms working to reduce their environmental impact; the Carbon Trust's Carbon Footprint, which shows the amount of greenhouse gases created in making a product; Conservation Grade, which certifies farmers devoting 10% of their land to nature-friendly habitats; and Freedom Food, the labelling scheme run by animal welfare charity RSPCA. RSPCA Freedom Food is a higher welfare alternative for people on a tight budget and means the animals have been reared in better indoor or outdoor systems with more space.

One of the most widely recognised marks — organic — is overseen by nine organisations worldwide and is upheld by Compassion in World Farming as the best for animal welfare. In Europe, food sold as organic must comply with the European Union's organic standards, which are among the strictest in the world. The main organic label in Britain is run by the Soil Association.

In the US, organic standards are regulated by the US Department of Agriculture, which has authorised 84 organisations to certify products as organic, 49 in the US and 35 in other countries. In 2012, the EU agreed to recognise the USDA organic standards as equivalent to its own but this was sharply criticised by Compassion in World Farming which says US organic standards on animal welfare are far lower than the EU standards. 'Not only would the US standards in some cases be considered non-organic in the EU, but some elements might even be deemed illegal on animal welfare grounds,' said Compassion's chief executive Philip Lymbery.

Here is some more detail about the definitions behind the labels (from the Soil Association and Compassion in World Farming):

Free-Range

Free-range eggs come from laying hens which have had access to the outdoors. Free-range meat chickens are given continuous access to an outdoor range during the daytime. In addition, they grow more slowly than intensive chickens, meaning that they tend to have better leg and heart health and a much higher quality of life.

There is no legal definition of 'free-range pork' across the EU but a voluntary industry code in Britain requires that free-range pigs have permanent access to pasture: born outside (without stalls or crates) and then reared outside throughout their lives.

When buying pig meat, Soil Association labels mean higher welfare. Other labels to be aware of are:

Organic

Organic food is produced using environmentally and animal-friendly farming methods on farms certified as 'organic'. These methods are legally defined and any food sold as 'organic' must be strictly regulated. Animals raised in organic systems enjoy the highest welfare standards of farmed animals. In Britain organic farm animals must:

- have access to fields (when weather and ground conditions permit) and are truly free range.

- have plenty of space.

- be fed a diet that is as natural as possible and free from genetically modified organisms.

- be given drugs to treat an illness — the routine use of antibiotics is prohibited.

- not be given hormones that make them grow more quickly or make them more productive.

- not be produced from cloned animals.

Outdoor Reared

Pork labelled as 'outdoor reared' means the piglets are born outside and spend around half of their lives outside. The sows are kept free-range, outdoors, with huts for both shelter and for having piglets. There are no sow stalls or farrowing crates and the huts are provided with straw. In these systems, sows have a higher quality of life and are able to act naturally by building nests, rooting, wallowing and foraging, and the piglets spend longer outside than those labelled as 'outdoor bred'.

Outdoor Bred

Pork labelled as 'outdoor bred' means that the sows are kept free-range, outdoors, and there are no sow stalls or farrowing crates. However, at weaning, the piglets are taken indoors and reared in extensive or intensive conditions. The piglets benefit from the free-range conditions until they are weaned.

No label

Meat with no welfare label has probably been kept in extensive or intensive conditions. Buyers beware: Because there is no legal definition of free-range pork, and therefore no policing of the provenance of the meat, some unscrupulous producers could use one of these labels as a marketing tool when in fact the meat has been produced in more intensive conditions than you might expect.

Where's This From? is a free app that gives shoppers more information on the food available in British supermarkets. Every packet of meat that is sold in supermarkets carries an oval European Union Identification Mark with a four-digit code that links to data published by the British Food Standards Agency on approved meat operators in Britain. The app tells you the name, location and activities of the operator (typically a slaughterhouse, cutting or packaging plant).

Download it from wheresthisfrom.com.

You Can't Make an Omelette Without Breaking an Egg...

One morning in 2005, ARC's director of communications Victoria Finlay was having breakfast at the Methodist International Centre (MIC) in Euston, London. The centre is a small Methodist-owned hotel that offers accommodation and conference facilities to visitors from all over the world.

She asked if the eggs they served were free-range; they weren't. Why not? She was told that it was too expensive. She then asked whether serving eggs from caged hens rather than from free-range birds accorded with Methodist beliefs and values about compassion. This challenge led to internal discussions about living according to one's beliefs, which resulted in a radical change in how the hotel operates. Today it is a model of ethical and environmentally conscious purchasing. It offers free-range eggs, high-welfare meat, and a wide variety of seasonal, fair-trade, organic and locally sourced produce on its menus.

Introducing these changes was not simple: when managers first asked its contract caterer to switch to using free-range eggs, it refused — too much hassle, it seemed, for this major London firm. So the hotel had to take all its guest and conference centre catering in-house, employing its own chefs and revamping its food-purchasing policy, to meet its own revised standards of ethical hospitality.

The hotel has also been working hard to transform all its operations — from energy use, waste, food sourcing and procurement — to be sustainable and environmentally friendly as well as consistent with its values and beliefs. In 2010 it became the first hotel in the UK to be awarded the prestigious Social Enterprise Mark and has also won a number of sustainability and green tourism awards.

In May 2013 MIC renamed itself The Wesley after John Wesley, who with his brother Charles is credited with founding Methodism. The move, The Wesley, says, was 'to reflect our pride in our Christian and Methodist heritage together with a passion for providing modern ethical hotel accommodation'. The aim is to 'protect and enhance the environment while minimising the impact of our business activities'. And underneath it all is an ethos of Christian care and duty.

The Big Beef
— About Meat

"It takes nearly 5,000 litres of water to produce one kilogram of pork. This is the equivalent of taking a 16-hour shower"

— Stuffed, *by Pat Thomas*

The way we feed ourselves is unsustainable. The challenges of obesity, rising food prices, degraded and destroyed ecosystems, waste, animal suffering, climate change, pollution, inequalities and unfair trading systems are the combined impacts of our unsustainable patterns of food consumption and production. Feeding a growing and more affluent global population healthily, fairly and sustainably simply isn't possible unless we make some changes.

We know there are no magic bullets. Reducing food waste and producing food with less impact on the environment are both essential but not sufficient. Modifying our consumption patterns must be a priority too.

One vital, simple step as part of this transition is for people in high-consuming countries to eat less meat — whether red, white or processed — and to eat more plant-based foods. We can do this by eating more meat-free meals, eating meat in smaller portion sizes, using small quantities of meat to add flavour or reserving meat for special occasions. We can also choose 'better' meat that is naturally fed, has a known provenance and is produced to high animal welfare, environmental and quality standards.

A 'less but better' approach to meat-eating can also help support farmers without being more expensive for consumers.

Eating Better: For a Fair, Green, Healthy Future is a new movement to raise awareness about how simple changes, such as reducing meat consumption in high-consuming countries can have positive benefits for public health, climate change, the environment and animal welfare, while also reducing pressures on land use and food prices. We want a culture where we place greater value on the food we eat, the animals that provide it and the people who produce it.

Our vision is a world in which everyone has access to healthy, humane and sustainable diets. In this world, meat will be produced humanely and sustainably, and consumed in quantities consistent with good health and the world's resources. Most people are familiar with advice to eat healthily and many are concerned about animal welfare, supporting fair trade, reducing food waste and seeking out more local, seasonal produce. Yet far fewer are aware of the impact of meat-rich diets on climate change, the environment and feeding the world fairly.

Britain's meat consumption is high compared with average global levels — approximately twice the world average. Yet we haven't always eaten so much. The shift away from naturally grazed livestock towards grain-fed, industrial production has resulted in cheaper meat, particularly chicken, but at a cost — to animal welfare, our health and the environment.

meat is a 'hotspot' for greenhouse gases

Changing our diets to include less meat and more plant-based ingredients will help reduce heart disease, obesity and cancer. Indeed, it has been calculated that eating meat no more than three times a

did you know?

Livestock production is a major driver of deforestation — cattle enterprises have been responsible for 65-80% of the deforestation of the Amazon, and countries in South America are clearing large swathes of forest and other land to grow animal feed crops such as maize and soybean.

week would prevent 45,000 early deaths a year in Britain and save the NHS £1.2 billion a year.

The food we eat carries a huge environmental footprint and meat is a 'hotspot' for greenhouse gas emissions, land and water use, pollution and biodiversity loss. According to the United Nations Food and Agriculture Organization, livestock production is responsible for around 18% of the world's greenhouse gas emissions and 30% of the world's biodiversity loss. Direct climate change impacts come largely from two powerful greenhouse gases: methane and nitrous oxide. Methane is released by livestock in their manure and, particularly, by ruminating cattle and sheep which exhale this gas during the digestive process. Nitrous oxide comes from nitrogenous fertiliser, other inputs applied to feed crops or grazing land, and the breakdown of animal waste.

Added to these are the indirect greenhouse gas emissions that can be attributed to animal feed such as soya, when land is converted from natural grassland or forest to agricultural use. The huge scale of land-use change in South America has been driven by cattle grazing and demand for soya crops. Soya is a common ingredient in concentrated animal feeds due to its high protein content. It is used particularly in pig and poultry production, as well as for dairy cattle. Growing global demand for meat and dairy products — predicted to double by 2050 — will only exacerbate these challenges.

The production of meat also requires vast quantities of water. On average, producing 1kg of beef requires 15,000 litres of water. Growing demand for grain for animal feed leads to competition for land and increases the price of staple foods. As grain prices continue to rise and people all over the world are struggling to feed themselves, it is right to ask whether we should be feeding so much grain to livestock instead of people.

feeding grain to livestock is inefficient

With over one-third of the global grain harvest and 97% of soymeal used for animal feed rather than feeding humans directly, meat and livestock is at the heart of the food security debate about how best to meet the world's food needs. Feeding grain to livestock rather than people is inefficient. To produce 1kg of meat by industrial methods takes 20kg of feed for beef, 7.3kg for pig meat and 4.5kg for chicken. As Bill Gates writes in *The Future of Food*: 'Raising meat takes a great deal of land and water and has a substantial environmental impact. Put simply, there's no way to produce enough meat for nine billion people.'

Photo credit: Wonderlane

We know that livestock raised on flower-rich pasture are happier and healthier; that the permanent pasture needed to feed grass-fed livestock sequesters more carbon than the ploughlands used to produce grain-fed meats; that ancient grassland helps to protect our water supplies.

Yet we sat by in the past 60 years or so as more than 97% of our meadowland has been extinguished, physically drained and ploughed out of existence, or force-fed a diet of herbicides and fertilisers like some luckless foie gras goose.

— *Andy Byfield, founder of charity* Plantlife

Yet many people in the Global South — particularly children — could benefit from more of the protein and micronutrients that meat and milk can provide in their diets. As the world's population continues to grow, it's vital that global consumption, including meat consumption, is re-balanced more equitably.

Part of the solution is to support more naturally grazed, grass-fed livestock production as this avoids many of the impacts of intensively produced, cereal-fed animals. Permanent pasture for grazing can act as a 'carbon sink' — this is a reservoir of carbon compounds which, left undisturbed, means fewer carbon emissions are released into the atmosphere. Research in 2011 by The Grasslands Trust (which has a vision that 'one day everyone in the UK will have a beautiful meadow close to their home') found meadows could be better at soak-

ing up carbon from the atmosphere than woodlands. Pasture-reared beef has also been found to contain less fat and a higher proportion of beneficial omega-3 fatty acids compared with intensively reared beef.

Eating Better recognises that raising livestock can be an efficient use of poor-quality farmland that could not otherwise grow crops. Keeping livestock on semi-natural habitats such as plant and wildlife-rich meadows and pastures is an important conservation tool and helps maintain valued landscapes. By thinking about how our meat is produced and making simple changes to the way we eat, we can help create a fairer, greener, healthier future.

Sue Dibb is co-ordinator of **Eating Better: For a Fair, Green, Healthy Future.**

'Let Humanity Entirely Abstain from Eating Flesh'

"You kill living beings and call it a righteous action. Tell me, brother, what would you call an unrighteous action? You call yourself the most excellent sage; then who would you call a butcher?"

– Bhagat Kabeer Ji, Sri Guru Granth Sahib, 1103

To be truly kind to animals we should stop eating them altogether. That's the view of some faith traditions that find the idea of killing and eating animals profoundly abhorrent. Religious opposition to eating meat has been strong among some schools of Buddhism, Hinduism, Jainism and Sikhism for centuries.

Buddhism's first precept is to avoid killing or harming living beings, for example, although not all Buddhists take this to mean they must follow a vegetarian diet.

Many Hindus also consider meat to be *tamasic* (influenced by ignorance). For them, *ahimsa*, or non-cruelty, is an important component of *dharma* — a life centred on good thinking and right living. As the Hindu sacred text, the Manusmriti, says: 'Having well considered the origin of flesh-foods, and the cruelty of slaying corporeal beings, let humanity entirely abstain from eating flesh.'

The refusal to kill and eat animals also has a long Christian tradition, says Deborah Jones of the Christian Vegetarianism Association UK: 'The early monastic movement embraced total abstinence from meat. The monks modelled their lifestyle on Jesus' 40-day sojourn in the wilderness, which he spent peaceably in the company of "the wild beasts".'

Around 1,700 years ago, St Ambrose said: 'We ought to be content to live on simple herbs, on cheap vegetables and fruits such as nature has presented to us and the generosity of God has offered to us.' His words are still relevant for today, says Deborah: 'Such a modest lifestyle would also be good for the environment and for enabling more of the world's poor to have enough to eat.'

The Christian Vegetarianism Association UK was founded in 2004 to promote 'compassion in action'. It believes 'the pain caused by our desire to eat the flesh of God's creatures stands out as one of the greatest sources of suffering in the world.' Its Veg4Lent campaign invites people to begin by giving up meat during Lent. In the UK in May 2011 Catholic Bishops in England and Wales re-introduced giving up meat on Fridays.

This moral debate of killing other beings is centuries old and now growing numbers of people of faith are beginning to reject meat-eating on environmental grounds as well, because of its greater impact on climate change.

Then God said, 'Look, I have given you every seed-bearing plant throughout the earth and all the fruit trees for your food.

And I have given every green plant as food for all the wild animals, the birds in the sky, and the small animals that scurry along the ground — everything that has life.'

– Genesis 1:29–30

the controversy over ritual slaughter

Jews and Muslims are required to eat meat that is ritually slaughtered according to religious rules governing kosher and halal food. But can ritual slaughter be considered humane? And if the animal is stunned beforehand to minimise distress, can this be considered kosher or halal?

This area is highly controversial, even within some Jewish and Muslim communities, as well as among animal welfare agencies. This is a specific process of slaughter, set out in great detail by each faith, in which an animal's throat is cut and it bleeds to death. It includes prayers that honour the life of the animal and therefore places the act of slaughter within the greater picture of Creation and thus of the Creator.

Jewish and Muslim slaughterers maintain their methods are humane because the procedure is swift and efficient, and carried out by highly trained people using surgically sharp instruments. This leads to the animal losing unconsciousness rapidly, they say. Critics say this does not always happen, however, and maintain that, in any case, the procedure causes suffering.

Organisations such as RSPCA and Compassion in World Farming believe all animals must be stunned before slaughter. Under Jewish and Islamic law, animals for slaughter must be healthy and uninjured at the time of death. This rules out stunning for many Jewish authorities, although some Muslim authorities accept some forms of stunning. In Britain, stunning is used for a high proportion of animals slaughtered for halal meat, but this is not the case for kosher meat.

Shechita UK, which promotes the Jewish religious slaughter method, criticises practices in conventional slaughterhouses as inhumane compared to ritual slaughter. These include captive bolt shooting, gassing, electrocution, drowning and clubbing, 'not to mention the many millions of animals who are "mis-stunned" every year, requiring them to be re-stunned,' it says. However, this issue is set to remain a flashpoint for controversy and high emotion on all sides.

There's no such Word as Can't

It is easy to take food for granted, even when we're talking about the environment and food sourcing. The following email exchange between ARC's Secretary General Martin Palmer and the Reverend Dr Alan Garrow of Bath Abbey also shows how easy it is to make significant changes. With thanks to Alan for letting us reproduce their conversation.

Martin was asked to deliver a sermon as part of the Christian Vision for the Environment service for Bath Abbey and its neighbour church of St Michael's in October 2013. This was to be followed by a harvest supper for around 150 people. Before the event, Martin asked about the provenance of the ingredients for the meal. 'I felt the food had to be consistent with what I would have just been talking about,' he says. 'How could I stand there talking to people about a better way of sourcing food and then share a meal which did not at least to some degree reflect the values and beliefs I had been talking about?'

From: Alan Garrow
Date: 8 October, 2013 13:59
To: Martin Palmer
Subject: **Food on Saturday evening**

Dear Martin,

A place where we have failed in relation to your suggestions and wishes is in the consistently ethical sourcing of the food for Saturday evening. I met with the organisers this morning and it is too late to change the arrangements they've made. A lesson learned for another year.

Best, Alan

From: Martin Palmer
Sent: 10 October, 2013 13:56
To: Alan Garrow
Subject: **Food**

Dear Alan,

I am working on the Saturday night presentation and need to just know one or two more details about the food. Is there anything in the food that reflects Christian values of care of creation? Is the chicken at least free range? Are the vegetables, or at least some of them, organic? Is the water from a tap not a bottle? Can you give me anything that shows the food reflects faithful living with the rest of God's Creation? Is there a vegetarian option? Hope to hear from you soon.

Martin

From: Alan Garrow
Sent: 10 Oct 2013, 14:43

Hi Martin,

I will put this question to those
who are organising the food and
get back to you. There is a vegetarian
option, and the chicken is free range…
I hope to have more to report shortly.

Alan

From: Martin Palmer
Sent: 10 October, 2013 15:08

Dear Alan,

Great to hear the chicken is free range. That
gives me a great starting point. Many thanks.

M

From: Alan Garrow
Sent: 10 October, 2013 17:03

Sorry for the dribs and drabs on this. The
bread is coming from the Thoughtful Bread
Company based in Bath. The apples will be
coming from people's gardens we trust (and
we know this in some cases). More to come
tomorrow.

Alan

From: Alan Garrow
Date: 11 October, 2013 13:52

Dear Martin,

The water will be from the tap. The chicken
is Waitrose Free-Range British. The bread
is from The Thoughtful Bread Company
— eco-artisan bakery based in Bath. The
plates are compostable — made from palm
leaves, I believe. The apples will be (mostly)
from people's gardens.

That's as much as I can muster.

Alan

Call to Action:
Sharing and Community

The Catholic Fund for Overseas Development (CAFOD) has long promoted a campaign for Catholics to 'Live simply so that others may simply live'. A *Live*simply Award is made to parishes that pledge to 'live simply, live sustainably with creation and live in solidarity with people living in poverty'. Brentwood Cathedral in England, which won the award in December 2013, held a *Live*simply week with different challenges every day 'from walking to Mass, to eating less meat, to making someone smile!' said co-ordinator Brenda Underwood.

did you know?

If everyone in the world consumed in the manner we do in Britain, we would need three planets' worth of resources to support us.

— One Planet Food Strategy,
WWF-UK

Small changes can
make big differences.

Commit to adopting one
of these ideas in your
daily life.

Action Points

🌱 Start a community orchard or garden on faith-owned land and share the harvest with the community.

🌱 Try to eat as a family as often as possible. As the old saying goes, families that eat together stay together.

🌱 Share the joy of celebrating good food in your wider community; institute regular potluck suppers or harvest feasts.

🌱 Link up with a vegetable box delivery scheme to have boxes delivered via your place of worship or faith community centre.

🌱 What about Community Supported Agriculture? Could your place of worship become involved or start some other form of direct-purchasing arrangement with local farmers and producers?

🌱 Why not invite members of another faith group, or other 'outsiders', to join one of your food-related events; for example, to share in your Eid meal or harvest festival?

🌱 Organise a debate in your community on food, social justice and the environment; for example, invite a local farmer to give a talk after a potluck supper.

🌱 What is the food culture in the local school? Ask questions through the Parent Teacher Association, interviewing the head-teacher or as a topic for governors to discuss. Where does the school's food come from? Could the school develop gardening or cooking clubs and put more about healthy/sustainable eating on the curriculum? How can those clubs be made to seem fun?

🌱 Twin with communities in parts of the world already suffering as a result of climate change.

🌱 Find out what position local councillors and political parties have on food and sustainability issues. Local authorities are major food buyers and thus could play a huge role in encouraging local producers, supporting Fairtrade and reducing environmental impact.

Photo credit ARC

Social Justice

"Some hae meat and
cannae eat. Some wad
eat that want it.

But we hae meat and
we can eat and sae the
Lord be thankit."

Translation:
"Some have meat and
cannot eat. Some
would eat but lack it.

But we have meat
and we can eat and
so let the Lord be
thanked."

– *The Selkirk Grace (an old Scottish blessing)*

Gambling on Hunger...

"God loves those who are fair and just"

– Qur'an 49:9

On a warm June morning in lower Manhattan in 2011, members of faith groups held a vigil in front of the New York Mercantile Exchange, calling on the United States Commodity Futures Trading Commission (CFTC) to rein in excessive speculation in food commodities and energy markets — speculation which contributes to worldwide hunger.

The group stood near the adjacent Irish Hunger Memorial, a patch of grass on which sits the ruins of a cottage built in the middle of Battery Park City to commemorate the Great Irish Famine of 1845–52. They held signs that read 'Stop gambling on hunger' and 'NYMEX: Where Wall Street gambles with our food and gas.' Vigil organisers said they chose the memorial for its proximity to the Mercantile Exchange, but also for the ironic juxtaposition it presents. One of the persons present at the vigil was Maryknoll lay missioner Dave Kane. Dave had worked in north-east Brazil for many years, and in 2011 was part of Maryknoll's advocacy efforts in Washington, DC, for peace, justice and the integrity of creation.

In early 2008, Maryknoll missioners began telling Dave that food prices were dramatically increasing in their countries and described how this was affecting the people they lived and worked with. Families that had previously bought large sacks of grains could now only buy smaller bags. Stores were dividing their kilogram bags of beans in half, or less, to make them affordable. This meant families were eating half or less than they used to before the crisis. People switched from healthier grains to cheaper ones that were poorer in nutritional value — only to see those prices rise too.

Dave started to look into the causes of these rising food prices and learned that it would be possible to reduce the high, unstable food prices that people around the world were experiencing just by bringing back laws to regulate commodities trading in the USA similar to those that had been in effect since the 1930s, but that had been weakened and eventually eliminated by 2000.

the link between food speculation and food prices

Commodities are the lifeblood of the global economy, the root of everything that is consumed, including food, which is the basis of life itself. In order to distribute commodities throughout the economy efficiently, their prices should be determined on the basis of conditions of supply and demand of each product. That is why, beginning with the Commodity Exchange Act of 1936, the US Congress established

rules in the commodity futures markets to allow producers and consumers of physical commodities to hedge safely. For a number of essential food commodities, Congress defined speculative position limits in order to allow traditional speculators to provide liquidity to the markets.

The function of traditional speculators is to predict future market patterns and therefore reduce the risk — that is, reduce volatility and stabilise prices. This system functioned fairly smoothly for many decades, but in the past 25 years, a series of steps taken by the CFTC and Congress have resulted in commodity futures markets where prices are not only determined by the supply and demand of physical commodities, but also by the whims of institutional investors.

Perhaps the beginning of the slippery slope was in 1986, when Congress asked the CFTC to expand exemptions from specu-

lation limits (traditionally applied to commercial firms hedging physical holdings of a commodity) to traders who deal in exotic financial derivatives known as 'swaps'. 'Swap dealers' can use the futures market to hedge their exposure to financial instruments rather than trading in actual physical commodities.

In addition, the CFTC allowed managers of exchange-traded funds to ignore speculation position limits, even though others still had to adhere to them. In 2004, the Securities Exchange Commission (SEC) permitted the first commodity index funds. These funds are essentially 'index traders' that focus on returns from changes in the index of a commodity. They periodically roll over commodity futures contracts prior to their maturity date and reinvest the proceeds in new contracts. They do not take physical ownership of the commodities involved.

Unregulated commodity exchanges allowed all investors, including hedge funds, pension funds and investment banks, to trade commodity futures contracts without

> *How can we remain silent when even food has become the object of speculation or is linked to a market that, without any regulation and deprived of moral principles, appears linked solely to an objective of profit?*
>
> – *Pope Benedict XVI, 2011*

any position limits or regulatory oversight and with minimal disclosure requirements. As the American housing finance market imploded in 2007, the market searched for new sources of profit. And many traders settled on commodity speculation. In 2002, speculators represented 20% of commodity market participants; by 2008 (by some estimates) they represented 89%. During those six years, the Food and Agriculture Organization's Food Price Index registered an average 83% price increase for essential foodstuffs, with an increase of 170% for rice alone. Later, food prices fell, but only to rise even higher in 2011.

According to Olivier De Schutter, the UN Special Rapporteur on the Right to Food: 'What we are seeing now is that these financial markets have developed massively

did you know?

Around 44 million people were plunged into poverty due to high food prices in 2010 and 2011, according to the World Bank.

what can be done to address this problem?

Regulators in the United States and the European Union have started to re-regulate the commodity markets. It is hoped that new rules will require trading to occur in regulated markets, impose strict limits on how much of one commodity any speculator can hold at one time and increase transparency of trading. It is striking that 82% of trading in European commodities is between two parties not registered on any trading exchange.

But the financial industry and its supporters are fighting these reforms. As De Schutter says: 'There is huge lobbying going on. These issues are so technical; lawmakers are literally running out of experts. They can only call on experts from the financial world. Very few legislators are well equipped to deal with these issues, which sometimes may be too technical for them to make relevant comments.

'It's really a problem of democracy. We are heading for a difficult situation: climate shocks, droughts, floods are increasingly frequent and extreme. The predictability of crop production is more difficult, so speculation is more attractive than ever, frankly. It is all the more important then, given this context of uncertainty, to regulate speculation to prevent things becoming even worse.'

with the arrival of these new financial investors, who are purely interested in the short-term monetary gain and are not really interested in the physical thing — they never actually buy the ton of wheat or maize; they only buy a promise to buy or to sell. The result of this financialisation of the commodities market is that the prices of the products respond increasingly to a purely speculative logic. This explains why in very short periods of time we see prices spiking or bubbles exploding, because prices are less and less determined by the real match between supply and demand.'

Increases in the price of food commodities (also heavily influenced by oil and gas prices due to the heavy dependence of our global food system on fossil fuels) affect those with lower incomes most heavily because they spend a higher portion of their income on food. In developing countries very low-income families are especially heavily affected because they often buy raw commodities in bulk, such as sacks of wheat and corn. So when the price of wheat triples, as it did between January 2005 and April 2008, the price of their food increases proportionally.

Catherine Rowan is Corporate Responsibility Co-ordinator for the Maryknoll Sisters, New York, USA.

Share your food
with the hungry.

– Isaiah 58:7

Eating is the Right of Everyone

"We in the West are using far more than our fair share of resources to feed ourselves. We are taking from the plates of others"

– Helen Browning, Soil Association Chief Executive

The common notion of justice entails giving everyone what is due to them. Yet to know what is due to everyone, we are required to have an eye to see and to recognise those who are in need. Recognising those in need obligates those who have something to share with those who do not. As long as a situation exists where some people have and others do not, injustice becomes our closest neighbour. Therefore, both in Christian Scripture and common traditional African wisdom and practices, the need to share, especially food, with those who do not have enough, is always emphasised.

Both in Scripture and common traditional African experience, food is first perceived as something that is given to us by God, who constantly takes care of all living things, including animals. Since food is first a gift to us, there is always enough to be shared. And so we know that food should be shared, especially with those who are hungry. Traditionally, a person on a journey, if hungry, can walk into someone's maize field and pick two or three cobs of corn to eat without having to ask for permission. This act is not considered stealing because the person on a journey is in need and they only take what they need. However, if they filled a bag with corn instead, without asking for permission to do so, then their act would be considered stealing. This understanding reflects a sense of both justice and religious consideration for a person in need.

There is a proverb in the Swahili language that says: '*Kula ni faradhi ya kila mtu*' — eating is the right of everyone. This implies that no one should go hungry. If eating is the right of all people, then we all have a moral obligation to ensure that those who do not have something to eat are also taken care of. In Luke 9:13, when Jesus' disciples recognise that the crowd needs something to eat, they ask Jesus to disperse the crowd. Jesus' response poses a challenge. Instead of dispersing the crowd, Jesus challenges the disciples: 'You yourselves give them something to eat.'

To recognise that another person is in need and to respond to that need manifests a sense of solidarity. In the spirit of solidarity, we have a moral responsibility to each other. We are one and we are a family. Hence in solidarity there is food for all and justice for all.

Brian Banda writes on issues of economic justice for the Jesuit Centre for Theology and Reflection, a CAFOD partner based in Zambia.

more money, more choice, more weight...

The epidemic of obesity, which is afflicting nations in North America and Europe, is also becoming a real problem in countries where people have moved away from traditional diets to so-called 'Western' diets which contain more fat, oils, sugar, meat and dairy.

A report released at the end of 2013 by a British think tank, the Overseas Development Institute, found that one in three people worldwide are now considered overweight — and one billion of them live in places such as China, the Middle East, North Africa, Mexico and Latin America.

That is four times the number classified as overweight in these countries in 2008.

Alan Dangour, a reader in food and nutritional global health at the London School of Hygiene and Tropical Medicine, says urban-

isation in many parts of the world has changed people's eating habits away from traditional, healthy diets. But he points out that obesity and under-nutrition often existed side by side, sometimes in the same household:

'We need to act urgently to deal with the scandal of millions of cases of extreme hunger and under-nutrition in children, but we also need to think what happens if we provide lots of extra calories, containing few vitamins, and encourage excess consumption.'

We Must Put Farmers First

"There is enough for everyone's need, but not for their greed"

— Mahatma Gandhi

The global food system is broken. Hunger, undernourishment and poverty continue to blight the lives of millions, while consumers in rich countries waste as much food as the entire net food production of sub-Saharan Africa[1]. Enough food for all should be within reach, but the solutions being offered by world leaders are falling far short.

There is a paradox at the heart of this discussion. Small farms grow most of the food eaten in developing countries. Yet more than half of the world's hungriest people are smallholder farmers themselves, and one-third of Africa's undernourished children live on small farms[2].

Most smallholders are trapped in a cycle of poverty from which they and their families have little power to escape alone. How can the immense potential for such farms to drive economic growth and reduce hunger be unlocked?

In 2009, the Fairtrade Foundation published a report — *The Global Food Price Crisis and Fairtrade: Small Farmers, Big Solutions* — which showed that smallholder farmers producing commodities such as coffee and cocoa were suffering as a result of high food prices. Even though world prices were high for these commodities, most such producers are net purchasers of food, so high staple food prices were cancelling out income gains from these higher commodity prices.

Our report highlighted the failure of governments and the private sector to invest in small-scale agriculture and sustainable farming practices as a key to future food security.

A Swedish farmhand will need to work for five minutes to earn enough to buy 1kg of cereals at the local market. A farmhand in India will have to work for 37 minutes — and a farmhand in the Central African Republic will need to work for six hours.

— Pope Benedict XVI, 2011

1   United Nations Department of Economic and Social Affairs Division for Sustainable Development Food and Agriculture, *The future of sustainability. Key Points for policy-makers*, March 2012.

2   P.Hazell et al, *The Future of Small Farms for Poverty Reduction and Growth*, IFPRI, 2007, p. 1

Fairtrade's expertise and experience is in working with farmers seeking to sell into local, regional or international markets, rather than subsistence agriculture, which require additional solutions. Our agenda focuses therefore on action to support the role that cash crops can play in supporting farmer livelihoods. We believe that by putting farmers first, ensuring fair share of value chains and fair access to finance, building future-proofed farming, and increasing the focus of government funding, should inform the policies and practices of governments, donors, multilateral agencies and private sector actors.

With the Fairtrade system already success-fully addressing many of the challenges faced by smallholder farmers, we argue here that Fairtrade is a vital part of the solution and that Fairtrade's values and driving principles justify much wider adoption in policies and initiatives involving smallholders.

Of course, we must listen hard to smallholder organisations themselves. It is they who know what the problems and solutions are, who pioneer improved farming practices, and who put their own money and working lives into growing staple food and commodities. Smallholder farmers are not a 'problem'; neither are they passive 'beneficiaries' of aid-driven solutions. If the power imbalances that hold smallholders back can be urgently addressed, and within supportive policy environments, they will drive down hunger and build prosperity for hundreds of millions.

Since then, both staple food and commodity prices have remained highly volatile. This puts the livelihoods of commodity producers at risk and threatens the food security of a huge number of people in the developing world, many of them smallholder farmers themselves. Around 44 million people were plunged into poverty due to high food prices in 2010 and 2011, according to the World Bank. International bodies such as the Food and Agriculture Organization predict that food prices are likely to remain high and volatile for the next decade, at the very least posing grave concerns for the future of smallholder farmers.

After decades of neglect, food security and smallholder agriculture has finally risen up the agenda of world leaders and institutions. There are new calls for reinvestment in small-scale farming and for more smallholders to be included in major supply chains.

Michael Gidney is Chief Executive Officer of the Fairtrade Foundation.

what is fair trade?

If all trade were conducted fairly, we wouldn't need a fair trade movement. But the reality is that too many farmers in poorer countries don't get a fair share of the wealth produced by trade. In some cases, that's because the rules of international trade favour richer countries. In others, it's because smallholder farmers are often at the end of a long chain of buyers and traders and have to accept whatever price is offered for their crops. As a result, farmers and farm workers often struggle to earn enough to provide for their families; wages are low, livelihoods fragile and working conditions hard.

The idea of ethical trade is not new. In the late 18th century a 'free produce movement' was launched by Quakers in Britain and the United States who called for a boycott of products made using slave labour, such as sugar, as part of their campaign against slavery. They argued that people buying these products were as culpable as slave owners in maintaining slavery, according to the **Encyclopedia of Antislavery and Abolition**.

In the 1960s the Oxford Committee for Famine Relief (which went on to become the international development organisation Oxfam) began selling handicrafts made in developing countries in its shops, giving producers a fair price for their goods, as a form of 'helping by selling' charity. The first fair trade labelling scheme was launched in Holland in the late 1980s where a brand of Mexican coffee called Max Havelaar was sold into Dutch supermarkets. It proved enormously popular and similar schemes spread to other countries.

Today, Fairtrade has become the most widely recognised ethical label in the world. In Britain, the mark is managed by the Fairtrade Foundation; globally, it is overseen by Fairtrade Labelling Organisations International. It is the only certification scheme whose purpose is to tackle poverty, by paying farmers a fair price for their products and by empowering farmers and workers in developing countries to take more control over their future. The extra premium earned by Fairtrade farmers enables them to invest in projects to improve their quality of life, such as schools, for example.

- More than seven million farmers, farm workers, and their families in Africa, Asia and Latin America benefit from Fairtrade.

- The Mexican coffee called Max Havelaar was followed by Green & Black's Maya Gold chocolate, Cafédirect medium roast coffee and three varieties of Clipper tea in 1994. Now more than 4,500 products carry the Fairtrade mark, including bananas, grapes, avocados, dried fruit, cakes, jams, rice, herbs and spices, wines, beers, ice cream, flowers, clothing, homeware and cosmetics.

- Sales of Fairtrade certified products have been growing at an average of 40 per cent per year over the last five years.

- Since launching in 2000, Fairtrade bananas now account for one in three bananas sold in the UK.

- Fairtrade products are sold in 125 countries.

– Figures from the Fairtrade Foundation

Thanks
a Bunch!

There are people in the Windward Islands who say Fairtrade has saved the islands' banana industry. Conrad James is one of them. He grows bananas on his five-acre farm for export to the UK.

He has seen first-hand how the islands' economy has suffered under trade rules that made it harder for his bananas to keep their place on British shelves against cheaper imports from Latin America. He believes people choosing Fairtrade do a great thing.

Conrad says: 'You help a community you don't know...that's marvellous.' And Fairtrade has helped Conrad's community. The premium the farmers receive for every box of bananas has been invested in fans for the local medical centre to keep patients cool and in improvements to the local school.

Consumers and Investors
Can Change the World

*"The superior being seeks what is right;
the inferior one, what is profitable"*

– Confucius

More than 30 years ago, after years of being concerned about hungry people, I became a vegetarian. I understood that a pound of grain goes further in feeding people than as animal feed for meat products. I'm moved by the story in Matthew of Jesus feeding the 5,000. My guess is that the miracle of this moment had more to do with inspiring these travellers to share the resources they had with them, rather than food appearing out of nowhere. Eating low on the food chain became my effort to share.

I soon realised the advantages were mine: a vegetarian diet was much healthier. While hunger continued to be a concern, I was not exposed to antibiotics and chemicals, or the high cholesterol, heart disease or diabetes that can arise from meat-eating. The macro issues became more serious: agribusiness grew, while family farms disappeared; outrageous use of pesticides and herbicides was enabled by genetically modified seed; sewage run-off from concentrated animal-feeding operations [highly intensive livestock farming] impacted water quality; the list seems endless. It's overwhelming. Being a vegetarian wasn't going to change systems, but as an investor and consumer, I had a chance.

In the late 1970s I began to work with a community of people who were changing economic systems. The US-based Interfaith Center on Corporate Responsibility (ICCR) and one of its members, the Tri-State Coalition for Responsible Investment (Tri-State CRI), were born in the anti-apartheid era when faith-based institutional investors used their power as shareholders and called upon companies to leave South Africa. These pioneers of socially responsible investing soon addressed companies on a spectrum of social and ecological issues. Economic systems held a key to the critical changes that were needed in society and for the Earth. Soon into my tenure in this interfaith setting, I realised that our traditions brought us together more often than apart. As we continue to share the diversity of our rituals, and create prayers that we can easily hold in common, we recognise the mutual passion for justice for all God's people and the sacredness of God's creation.

responding to the holy

Colleagues in financial management firms, public pension funds, human rights and environmental NGOs, and corporate executives are invited into this challenging space. This collaboration holds an invitation to all in our work to respond to the Holy in both personal and collective ways. ICCR members have always been passionate about

Photo credit: Matthew Jellings

access to healthy food. As mothers in the developed world returned to breastfeeding, infant formula companies looked to the developing world for new markets. Infant mortality rates rose as poverty prevented the safe use of formula. ICCR members filed shareholder resolutions with Nestle, Abbott, American Home Products, among others, until companies signed the 1981 International Code of Marketing of Breast-milk Substitutes.

With the growth of agribusiness, consumers grew further from the source of their food and knew less about how it was grown.

In the late 1980s, as food irradiation was introduced to increase shelf life, investors approached companies. Within two years, major food companies such as Heinz and restaurants including McDonald's developed policies that excluded the use of irradiated foods or ingredients.

Simultaneously, Monsanto introduced genetically modified (GM) seeds. In hindsight, ICCR members should have raised concerns about these new life forms before there was major investment by companies. There is still no evidence assuring the long-term safety for humans, while we witness serious environmental damage resulting from the increased use of herbicides necessitated by GM seeds. Our work with Monsanto, DuPont and Dow, as well as targeted companies such as PepsiCo and Campbell's, has focused on material and reputational risks related to the impact on human health and the environment. We now focus on labelling of GM products.

ICCR members prod companies on specific concerns under the umbrella of sustainability in the food supply chain, such as sustainable seafood, use of gestation crates and non-therapeutic antibiotics in animal breeding, sustainable palm oil, and the agricultural impacts on water. We work with companies on the abuses of human labour in the global food supply chain, as well as on access to nutrition.

driven by the sacredness of God's creation

In a different industry, we ask the financial sector to end excessive speculation in food commodities. Complex commodity investment products have contributed to severe volatility in food prices, contributing to spikes in the cost of food, creating deeper poverty and leaving people at greater risk of hunger and malnutrition.

This work extends to food companies impacted by this volatility. Investors are now directing managers to exclude these products that hold potential danger for poor people.

Coinciding with the emergence of the faith-based socially responsible investor movement, most faith traditions embraced the growing scientific evidence of the emergence of this planet. We now know that the cosmos is 13.8 billion years old. As we stand in awe of our planet's 4.54 billion-year journey, we are thrown into the depths of God's creative mystery. We are also thrown into the threats to God's creation.

Driven by this deeper understanding of the sacredness of God's creation, and the concerns of scientists and economists about the rapid shifts in climate, ICCR and Tri-State CRI members initiated our global-warming work in the late 1980s.

It was clear to us then that poor and vulnerable people would be most affected by climate disasters. It was also clear that the very commons that we rely on for sustenance were at risk. As food and water are elements used in the rituals of most faith traditions, it was an easy shift for us to embrace food, water, and the complexities of biodiversity into our priorities.

In 1980, while my attention was focused on companies impacting food systems, my Caldwell Dominican Sisters founded Genesis Farm. This project emerged as we were beginning to understand the impact of air, water, and soil pollution on the Earth, while the family-farm crisis with its consequent effects of malnourishment and world hunger was becoming evident.

The Caldwell Dominicans believe that the survival of the human species must be considered within the broader context of how Nature is surviving. The educational, ecological and agricultural work of Genesis Farm is rooted in a belief that the Universe, Earth, and all reality are permeated by the presence and power of that ultimate Holy Mystery that has been so deeply and richly expressed in the world's spiritual traditions.

*consumers make a
statement each time
they buy food.*

People want to know how their food is grown, support local farmers and participate in an agricultural system that reduces greenhouse gas emissions by buying locally. Consumers make a statement each time they buy food. Fair treatment of farm workers and payment of a living wage are important elements of our food systems. The growth of farmers' markets reflects people's commitment to healthy food choices.

People of faith, consumers and investors have changed the world. Our choices make us powerful. Every investor, institutional or individual, can participate. You can join with socially responsible investors in a variety of ways, especially through proxy voting.

Our Tri-State CRI welcomes individual investors and supporters as partners. Join a community-supported agriculture group, or shop at your local farmer's market. Ask for options that are organically grown or deemed sustainable. If you live in a country that permits GMOs, support product labelling.

You have the right to know. Or become a vegetarian. It opens your eyes.

Photo credit: Wade Sisler

sharing in the harvest

Genesis Farm founded one of the first community supported agriculture (CSA) gardens in the US. Using biodynamic agricultural methods, shareholders were assured of food grown from non-GM seed and without chemical pesticides. The food tasted different. A community was born as families supported farmers and upfront costs, while sharing in the harvest — a sacred enterprise. Today there are thousands of CSAs across the world.

Sister Patricia A. Daly OP is Executive Director of the Tri-State Coalition for Responsible Investment.

Greening Food in Houses of Worship

The world's faith groups increasingly recognise that protecting the Earth is a religious duty — and that this must start with their own land, property, purchasing — and food. The American religious environmental movement GreenFaith helps religious institutions and people of all faiths put their belief into action for the Earth. It has put together six steps for getting started in your house of worship and we've adapted them to help you 'green' the food provided in your own church, synagogue, mosque or temple.

❧ **Form a Green Team.** This is a critical first step; Green Teams help to keep your institution's environmental efforts strong, focused and continually moving forward.

❧ **Show a food/environmental film.** Possible examples include *Food Inc.* and *Our Daily Bread.* This is a great way to give your community an inside glimpse into environmental problems — and the good work being done in response to them.

❧ **Publish food-related eco-tips** in your newsletter or worship bulletin. This is really useful in helping your members recognise environmental stewardship as a religious responsibility, and thus taking steps to think about the food they eat, buy and grow.

❧ **Look at the food you are providing** in your own house of worship. If you serve tea or coffee after worship, where does it come from? Is the wine served as part of the Christian Mass fair trade, or the food, fruits and sweets offered during *puja* (prayer ritual) sustainably sourced? Many congregations can take significant steps to make their food and drink more sustainable. Be sure to publicise the environmental and financial success of your efforts in your newsletter, on your website and to the local media.

❧ **Conduct an educational series.** This builds awareness and helps identify interested leaders for your Green Team. You could start with GreenFaith's free *Splendor* series on faith and creation which focuses on the religious/spiritual basis for environmental work, the effects of our consumption, and environmental justice, to create wider understanding for why making our food more planet friendly is a faith issue.

❧ **Preach a 'green' sermon,** focusing on food and farming. Whether delivered by your ordained leader or a guest speaker, this sends a clear message to members that caring for how our food is produced and consumed is a religious value. The worship resources on GreenFaith's website provide references to sacred texts, as well as guidelines for developing an eco-themed service. And of course make sure that the coffee and cakes served afterwards are eco-friendly.

Sharing a Meal with Friends

Friends' House, the London headquarters of the Quakers, has a basketful of awards that demonstrate its commitment to ethical and sustainable business. Its popular restaurant and café have both been recognised by organisations including the Vegetarian Society Food & Drink Guild, Compassion in World Farming, the Sustainable Restaurant Association, the Soil Association, the Vegan Society and the Marine Stewardship Council.

All these accreditations and awards mean diners at the welcoming café, where custom has increased from 20,000 visitors in 2008 to 100,000 in 2013, can be confident that the food and drink on the tempting menu has been carefully sourced with environmental issues in mind. A sign outside the restaurant tells diners clearly why they've taken this trouble: it is to be faith-consistent.

Quakers (also known as the Religious Society of Friends) are increasingly expressing their concern for the environment and are aware of the unfairness of the consumer society and the unsustainable use of natural resources. Sustainability is a key part of Quakerism — of 'living what we believe', says Alison Prout of Quaker Peace & Social Witness in Britain. That's why Friends House has undergone a £1.6 million refurbishment to help it reach its target of reducing carbon emissions by 45% by 2015, with solar panels, recycled furniture and floor-coverings made from recycled bottle tops.

In August 2011 Quakers in Britain committed 'with joy' to become a low-carbon, sustainable community, saying: 'The time to act is now. We need to reduce the amount of carbon we produce. We are called to challenge the values of consumer capitalism.' The words 'with joy' are important, says Alison: 'This states explicitly that this decision was taken positively. This has not been done with a reluctant "Oh, we have got to do something" attitude. This reflects the fact that everybody has taken this on as being a joyful process. It became clear at the Yearly Meeting that the mood was for a really big commitment.'

This challenging decision calls on all Quakers in Britain to reduce their carbon footprint and to build a more sustainable society and economy. 'The Quaker testimonies of truth, integrity, justice, equality, community, peace and simplicity are lived experiences and not just a set of rules laid down in 1652 [at the founding of the Quaker movement],' says Alison. 'We are taking simplicity further. We have to ask ourselves what these things mean today.'

Great Idea!

Is Yours a
'Cool Congregation'?

US-based Interfaith Power & Light was set up in 2000 to mobilise a religious response to global warming. To date it has inspired more than 14,000 congregations from all faiths and denominations to take action through its Cool Congregation programme.

Here are some of their stories:

The Vestry of Grace Episcopal Church in Chattanooga, Tennessee, has transformed its two-acre grounds from an unused grassy field into a community garden.

The church felt its land should embody our relationship with the natural world and should provide an urban oasis for all life, for the greater glory of God.

Volunteers built 18 vegetable beds over two weekends. One was for the three Sunday School classes to teach children about gardening. The remaining 17 were taken up within ten days by both congregants and community members. The church serves a poor part of Chattanooga and rental is kept low ($20 per year).

The gardens are pesticide-free and watered by hand, and two to three inches of organic mulch are applied to reduce water needs. Plant waste is recycled into compost and free classes have been held in composting, garden

insects and diseases, home freezing and canning, and beekeeping.

Inspired by what happened *after* the feeding of the 5,000 — 'After everyone was full, Jesus told his disciples, "Now gather the leftovers, so that nothing is wasted".' (John 6:12) — Glenn Memorial United Methodist Church in Atlanta, Georgia, has transformed its composting practices.

Every October, the church holds a pumpkin sale, with families returning year after year to buy their Hallowe'en pumpkins. Inevitably a number of pumpkins are left over, and in the past they were destined to rot in rubbish tips.

Now all are composted, along with the pumpkins returned by parishioners after the festival, resulting in more than one ton of wet organic material being saved from landfill (where it generates carbon emissions) and used to improve soil health instead. Food scraps from other events — Wednesday Night Suppers, picnics on the lawn, Commitment Sunday lunches

— are also composted, and reusable or compostable cups and dinnerware are now used, to reduce waste.

Composting is spreading quickly to members' homes. It is getting to the point where composting is as common as recycling at Glenn, say church leaders. Other initiatives include an organic meal hosted with food from the local organic farmer's market. A local farmer from Truly Living Well Urban Farms came to help draw out the connections between what people were eating and a social and environmental perspective.

Temple Emanuel in Greensboro, North Carolina, has installed 24 solar panels, which generate electricity that is sold to a local power company for approximately $1,000 each year. More importantly, this green electricity prevents an estimated 8,000 lbs of coal from being removed from mountaintops and saves some 14,000 lbs of

Great Idea!

greenhouse gasses from being released into the atmosphere annually, says the temple's Teva Committee, which led the initiative.

The project was inspired by the Jewish concept of *Tikkun Olam* (repairing the world). Project chair Gary Silverstein says: 'Our enthusiasm is generated from our commitment as members of Temple Emanuel, our Greensboro community, our nation and our planet. All this we understand, respect and celebrate through our covenant and dedication as Jews, and as shared inhabitants of God's Green Earth.'

Other Teva initiatives include a recycling programme, a Mitzvah Garden which provides fresh vegetables to local food banks, a composting system that turns their kitchen scraps into fertiliser for the Mitzvah Garden, and a campaign to reduce the temple's reliance on disposable products in favour of reusable options.

Food and Worship in Sikhism

"Make love the farm, purity the water, truth and contentment the cows and bulls; humility the plough, consciousness the ploughman, remembrance the preparation of the soil, and union with the Divine the planting time."

– *Sri Guru Granth Sahib, 955*

Photo credit: Sarah Jamerson

Food as a Divine Gift

"Whatever one plants in the farm of the body, that will appear before him in the end"

— *Sri Guru Granth Sahib (SGGS), 1417*

Food is part of the spiritual life of every Sikh, and is commonly referred to as *rijak*, divine sustenance, or *giras*, nourishment. According to Sikh thought, after creating the Creation, the Divine continuously nourishes it and sustains it through breath and food. As the third Sikh Guru, Guru Amar Das writes in Sikhism's central religious text, Sri Guru Granth Sahib: 'The Creator created the creation; the Creator gazes upon it, and blesses it with breath and nourishment' (SGGS, 1055).

The Gurus remind us that constant nourishment by the Creator enables us to maintain a healthy mind and body, which we treat as a temple for the Divine. A person who is spiritually attuned eats according to need, avoiding overindulgence. The Gurus laid great emphasis on the state of mind with which we accept the blessings of this world, living in harmony with the Divine, as seen in this verse: 'While laughing, playing, dressing, and eating, one is liberated' (SGGS, 522).

They remind us that even in the normal activities of our lives, we can attain union with the Divinity contained in one's own self. It is through eating as well as drinking, playing, and laughing that we achieve union with our Inner Master, the highest power contained in all.

During the time of the Sikh Gurus, who lived and taught between 1469 and 1708, Sikhs who lived in rural areas often specialised in agriculture and artisanship, while those living in towns and cities excelled in trade and commerce. For all kinds of work, the Sikh Gurus narrated three basic principles to daily living:

- **Naam Japna**, living consciously with the Divine;

- **Kirt Karna**, ethical and honest work;

- **Vand Chakna**, sharing one's earnings with others.

So central are the ideas of ethical living and honest work that all the ten Gurus tried to exemplify them throughout their lives. Today, Sikh children are taught that the best food is that which is made with pure intention.

Food Production

The Gurus used the language of the people to communicate how to live a harmonious life in this world. While speaking to farmers, the fifth Guru, Guru Arjan, used the metaphor of cultivating land with one's own hands to describe union with the Beloved:

'By Your Command, the month of Saawan (monsoon season) has come.

I have hooked up the plough of Truth, and I plant the seed of the Name in hope that the Lord, in His Generosity, will bestow a bountiful harvest.'

– (SGGS, 73)

did you know?

Sikh gurdwaras provide free vegetarian food to an estimated 30 million people every day.

According to the Sikh Gurus, righteous living in honest labour, with one's mind attuned to the Divine, will render a bountiful harvest.

While intensive farming has come under greater scrutiny in recent years, through the heavy use of genetically modified seeds, chemical fertilisers and pesticides, and farm machinery, Sikh thoughts continue to encourage us to marvel, and be in awe of and to live in harmony with Creation, for it is only the Divine that knows the true nature of the created Universe.

As the first Guru, Guru Nanak says: 'Nature is created by the Will of the Divine. The Divine knows best and having created everything complete. The Divine has left no process incomplete.' The Sikh Gurus remind us that humans are unique, yet we do not have the right to exploit nature. Since the Earth is created by the Divine, everything has the right to live, exist and flourish. To destroy or exploit Creation would be tantamount to exploiting or disrespecting the Creator.

Photo credit: Meena Kadri

Ravneet Pal Singh and **Bandana Kaur.**

Ravneet Pal Singh is India programme manager for EcoSikh, a Sikh environmental movement launched in July 2009.

langar: a food system based on compassion

One of the most important traditions in Sikhism is Guru Ka Langar, the community kitchen. In every *gurdwara*, or temple, there is a kitchen, open to all regardless of caste, creed, gender, social standing or need. The tradition was not intended to be a symbolic gesture of charity, but to fully involve all who came to the gurdwara in the cultivation and provision of food.

In the times of the Sikh Gurus (from the late 15th to early 18th centuries), all who sought the Guru's guidance would first receive a lesson in the oneness of humanity, through sitting together on the ground enjoying a basic meal with others. This sharing of food would embody the two traditions of *sangat* (the ennobling influence of people who meet in a shared aspiration toward truthful living) and *pangat* (the family of humanity, sitting together and serving one another). In doing this, the Sikh Gurus placed more importance on our common humanity than the barriers of caste, creed, class, age, gender or any other divisions that come between people.

Soon, farmers became accustomed to bringing the first crop from their fields — whether wheat or fruit — to their nearby gurdwara. Today, in Punjab and many parts of South Asia, langar is offered daily in nearly all gurdwaras; around 65,000 eat at Sri Harmandir Sahib, the Golden Temple in Amritsar alone, and in total 30 million people around the world are estimated to receive free food from gurdwara kitchens every day. In order to make the food acceptable and delicious to the widest possible number of people langar is traditionally vegetarian.

Today langar kitchens are looking at issues such as composting, waste disposal, and using biofuel or solar energy instead of wood, so they do not produce unnecessary waste.

Photo credit: ARC

'Bought with Money Sucked Unfairly from the Poor'

A story told around the life of Guru Nanak tells how the best food is not about the richness of the ingredients, but the pureness of the intention.

It is told to every Sikh child:

The first Sikh Guru, Guru Nanak Dev ji travelled to many places, including Saidpur, now known as Eminabad, in to-day's Pakistan. Even before Guru ji had arrived at Saidpur the word had spread that a spiritual man was going to visit.

When Malik Bhago, the chief of the town, heard of the Guru's arrival he started preparing for him to stay at his home.

But Malik Bhago had amassed his wealth through charging extra tax to the poor farmers and leaving them hungry. And when Guru Nanak reached Saidpur, he did not go to the chief's house.

Instead he knocked on the door of a poor carpenter named Lalo, asking him for hospitality. Lalo was joyful, and served Guru ji with the little food that he had.

Malik held a big gathering and invited all the well respected, people of the town. But Guru ji did not accept his invitation.

Malik ordered two guards to go to Lalo's home to force the Guru to accompany them, and the Guru went as asked. When he arrived with the guards, Malik said to him: 'O devout one, I have prepared so many delicious dishes for you, but you are staying with a poor carpenter and eating his dry chapattis. Why?' And the Guru replied: 'I cannot eat your food because it has been bought with money sucked unfairly from the poor, while Lalo's bread is bought with his own hard work.'

This made Malik furious and he asked the Guru to prove his point. Guru ji then sent for a loaf of bread from Lalo's house. In one hand the Guru held Lalo's bread and in the other that of Malik, and he squeezed both. Milk dripped from Lalo's bread but from Malik's came blood.

The chieftain was shaken by guilt and asked for forgiveness. The Guru asked him to distribute his ill-gotten wealth among the poor and live an honest life, which he did from then on.

Sikh Dietary Rules

The Sikh religion began in the Punjab region in India in the 15th century under the teachings of Guru Nanak, who underlined the equality of all, service to the community and devotion to God. There are 24 million Sikhs worldwide. More than 90% live in India, mainly in Punjab.

Sikhs are expected to eat simple food and avoid alcohol and drugs that are considered to interfere with meditation and spiritual awareness. There is a long tradition of vegetarianism among some Sikh traditions, which includes not eating eggs, but there are no actual restrictions on eating meat — except for one. According to the official *Rehat Maryada* (code of conduct), the only absolute rule about eating meat is to avoid ritually slaughtered meat (halal or kosher).

Though eating meat is a personal choice of every Sikh, it is certainly a Sikh understanding that humanity should be kind to animals and not use them for greed or exploitation.

The Gurus were not alive when mass-production and industrial agricultural techniques were introduced, but a Sikh's personal choice should reflect 'kindness to Creation', says EcoSikh's Ravneet Singh.

Hence, a simple diet based on kindness to Creation and ethical production is one that will offer true sustenance to a Sikh. As Guru Arjan Dev wrote:

'Being kind to all life — this is more meritorious than bathing at the 68 sacred shrines of pilgrimage and the giving of all kind of charity.

'That person, upon whom the Divine bestows Mercy, is a wise person.'

– (SGGS, 136)

Sikh prayer

O Nanak, the Guru is the tree of contentment,

with flowers of faith, and fruits of spiritual wisdom.

Watered with the Lord's Love, it remains forever green;

through the karma of good deeds and meditation, it ripens.

– Sri Guru Granth Sahib, 147

Sikh Festival Food

Meethe Pakode

Diwali: For Sikhs, the festival of Diwali, also celebrated by Hindus and Jains, is particularly important because it celebrates the release from prison of the sixth guru, Guru Hargobind, and 52 other princes, in 1619.

Sweet fried dumplings such as Meethe Pakode are very popular at this time. This recipe uses jaggery, an unrefined sugar made from sugar cane juice that has been boiled and left to set. Buy it from Indian or South Asian stores, or order online.

Ingredients

(Use planet friendly, fairly traded, free-range ingredients wherever possible.)

150g / 5 and a half oz / 1 cup wheat flour

200g / 7oz jaggery

240ml / 8fl oz / 1 cup water

1 tbsp of fennel seeds

Oil for cooking

Method

Combine the jaggery and water until the whole jaggery is melted. Add flour and mix well until the mixture is smooth. Set the mixture aside for two hours.

Add the fennel seeds to the mixture and stir thoroughly.

Take a kadhai (a circular, cast-iron cooking pan similar to a wok) and add enough oil to fry the pakodes. Once the oil is hot, drop in one tablespoon of the mixture. You can cook four to five at the same time.

After one minute turn the pakodes over so both sides cook evenly. Once they are evenly browned, remove from the pan, drain the excess oil and serve.

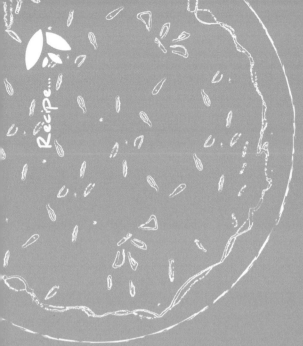

Jaggery Rice

Vaisakhi: Vaisakhi is Thanksgiving Day for Punjab farmers, when they thank God for the abundant harvest and also pray for future prosperity. For Sikhs it is of particular importance because it commemorates the forming of the **Khalsa** by the tenth and last living Guru, Guru Gobind Singh, in 1699, to take on the temporal leadership of the Sikh faith after his death.

Among the many popular dishes eaten at this festival (which is also New Year for Hindus) is jaggery rice. You can buy jaggery (unrefined sugar) from Indian or South Asian stores, or order online. This recipe has been supplied by Satvir Kaur, via the EcoSikh team.

Ingredients

(Use planet friendly, fairly traded, free-range ingredients wherever possible.)

200g / 7oz / 1 cup basmati rice (washed and soaked for 30 mins)

300 g/ 10 and a half oz jaggery

4 green cardamom pods

3 cloves

50ml / 3 tbsp cooking oil

950ml / 32 fl oz / 2 pints water

Method

Put the water into a small saucepan and bring to the boil. Add the drained rice, cloves and cardamom pods.

Bring to the boil, lower the heat and simmer until the rice is cooked. Drain the rice in a colander.

Heat the oil in a saucepan. Add the rice and mix well. Lower the heat and stir in the jaggery.

Cover and place the pan on a griddle over a low heat for about 15 minutes, stirring a couple of times. Serve hot.

making Sikh celebrations green

Food and drink is a key feature of many Sikh religious festivals which often draw large crowds of worshippers.

The EcoSikh movement has the following advice to help Sikhs green their festivals.

Each year, Vaisakhi celebrations bring together tens of thousands of Sikhs in cities all around the world in **nagar kirtans** (religious processions) to celebrate the birth of the Khalsa in Anandpur Sahib, Punjab, in 1699.

Vaisakhi celebrations are a time of immense joy for Sikhs. However, the introduction of modern-day packaging such as plastics and Styrofoam means that a lot of waste can be left behind.

Being non-biodegradable, these materials can last hundreds of years. They are bad for our health, and pollute our land, water, and air.

how can you make your local nagar kirtan green?

- Talk to the nagar kirtan organisers and ask them to use traditional, biodegradable leaf-plates pattals — or plates made from recycled paper, or plant- or clay-based materials for cups and utensils.

- Create a volunteer team to carry around recycling bags for plastic and glass. Wear green shirts or matching clothing. Make it fun. Talk to Sikhs about the importance of recycling and what you are doing.

- Make sure all stallholders have rubbish bins beside their stalls, and that they understand what you are doing and why.

- Set up a table at the nagar kirtan with information on Sikhism and the environment, and decorate it with greenery and a banner to reinforce the message.

Photo credit: EcoSikh

207

One Tonne of Daal, Two Hundred Thousand Rotis...

Amritsar, in north-west India, is Sikhism's most sacred site, home to the Sri Harmandir Sahib, or Golden Temple, built in the 16th century, which houses the original, handwritten copy of the Guru Granth Sahib, the holy book of Sikhism.

Each day around 100,000 visitors from all over the world come to the Golden Temple — that's 30 million visits each year. They make devotional offerings in the temple and bathe in its holy waters and around 65,000 of them share in the communal meals freely provided to everyone in accordance with Sikh customs of hospitality. This involves cooking at least one tonne of daal (lentil soup) and baking 200,000 rotis (Indian flat bread) every day.

In 2011, Amritsar became one of nine cities and 22 organisations that founded the Green Pilgrimage Network, which aims to help sacred places become more sustainable.

It committed to providing organic and pesticide-free food as well as safe drinking water for the millions of pilgrims that are fed each year.

Plastic water bottles have been banned and water stations, staffed by volunteers as part of the Sikh principle of service, set up to provide visitors with clean, fresh water. Plastic bags are also banned, and the Golden Temple has introduced several eco-rickshaws (powered by cycling rather than motors) to reduce traffic pollution.

It has pledged to expand the programme of giving out saplings for pilgrims to plant — ten million have been given already — and to celebrate Diwali with fewer fireworks. It has also committed to organic farming in the lands associated with gurdwaras in Amritsar district.

Some solar power is already used to heat water for cleaning plates and cutlery but there are plans to install a sophisticated solar cooking system for the Golden Temple's Langar Hall. This will halve the number of gas cylinders and greatly reduce the amount of wood — currently more than 30 tonnes per day — used to prepare meals in the Langar Hall.

Call to Action:
Wisdom and Learning

Case Study

Every year, the Uganda Supreme Muslim Council — the body leading Uganda's six million Muslims and 8,000 imams — dedicates a day to preaching on the environment and encouraging tree planting. Greening Friday is held on the second Friday of Ramadan, the holy month of fasting and prayer that is regarded as one of the five pillars of Islam.

The sermon is broadcast live via the National Mosque's radio station and tree seedlings are handed out to worshippers and planted at the Central Mosque by the Chief Imam himself. Since 2010, more than 30,000 seedlings, mainly fruit trees, have been distributed and every year demand for seedlings grows.

Muslims believe there is a special blessing to be obtained in planting trees — particularly those that provide food for humans or animals. This is known as *sadaqah jariyah* — a form of charity that provides everlasting rewards for as long as people benefit from your good deeds.

did you know?

The Southern African Faith Communities' Environment Institute runs an Eco Congregations programme helping 36 churches and mosques link their beliefs to practical action to care for creation.

Small changes can make big differences.
Commit to adopting one of these
ideas in your daily life.

Action Points

- All faiths regard food as a gift of the divine. If you have lost it, revive the tradition of saying grace before meals in gratitude and appreciation.

- Find out what your theological teachings say about food, farming and caring for creation. Can you collect them together and create a simple resource to be used by members of your community?

- Check out faith-based websites and resources on sustainable food, such as Christian Ecology Link, Hazon, EcoSikh, Green Muslim and the Bhumi Project. For example, the Jewish environmental group Hazon has produced **Food for Thought**, a sourcebook on Jews, food and contemporary life; the Jewish Greening Fellowship is an American programme to help synagogues become more sustainable; Interfaith Power & Light has a **Cool Harvest** programme; GreenFaith has **Repairing Eden**, a guide to sustainable food for houses of worship; and the Muslim campaigning group MADE in Europe has the Green Up! Awards for mosques.

- Understand the connection between traditions such as **tithing** (the Christian practice of giving one tenth of your income to good causes), **tzedekah** (Jewish charitable giving), **sewa** (Hindu or Sikh service of time or donations) or **zakat** (Islamic obligatory giving) to current approaches to philanthropy such as food banks or development charities. Can you donate or volunteer?

- Ask informed lay people to help your religious group better understand the importance of environmental issues. For example, ask someone from a local transition network, or a local farmer, to speak to your community.

- Organise film screenings followed by group discussions to help your faith community better understand issues around food and sustainability. Possible films include: **Food Inc**, **Fast Food Nation**, **Our Daily Bread**, **Super Size Me** and **Black Gold**, which is about the Ethiopian coffee trade.

- Cultivate a learning community within your religious organisation — share ideas, recipes and inspiration relating to faith, food and the environment.

- Learn how to make jams, pickles, chutneys and other ways of preserving seasonal foods.

- Build up a 'green map' or directory of local producers, retailers, cafés and other businesses offering sustainable foods and share it with others.

- Contact local schools — offer to give talks or assemblies on the subject of food and faith.

Food and Worship in Buddhism

Photo credit: Monks Community Forest, Cambodia

"May this food be dedicated to the triple jewel

The precious Buddha

The precious Dharma

The precious Sangha

Bless this food so we may take it as medicine

Free from attachment and desire

So that it may nourish our bodies so we may work for the benefit of all sentient beings."

— *Buddhist Prayer*

Humans Don't Need to Eat Meat

"My religion is very simple; my religion is kindness"

— *The 14th Dalai Lama Tenzin Gyatso*

Shakyamuni Buddha says in the Karmavibhanga Sutra:

'In this regard, there are actions extending life. What are they? To give up killing, to praise giving up killing, to encourage others to give up killing, to save the lives of those sure to be killed or supposed to be killed such as humans, cattle, goats, sheep, fish, pigs, birds, game, and so on....

'To protect from fear beings oppressed by it, to generate compassion towards those who do not have a protector, to generate loving kindness towards the sick, towards children, and towards the elderly, to give them food, medicine, and so on, to generate compassion towards beggars, as well as preventing war, and the like.'

Similarly, the Dalai Lama has said:

'Being kind to animals, saving them, and protecting them is not a matter of religion... It is something everyone should do.'

Except for a few cultures and religions, and some people who naturally don't eat meat, most of the world has the bad habit of eating meat without analysing this practice. If we analyse the details, humans don't need to eat meat. Their natural body system is not like tigers, snakes or lions. Humans don't have fangs.

According to Buddhist cosmology, the Abhidharmakosha says that at the beginning of this Earth, countless years ago, our lineage grandfather Bramah and the gods and goddesses were miraculously reborn. They had light and were able to fly. They didn't eat dirty food, meat, egg or blood. They used concentration food and nectars.

Many years later, some gods and goddesses ate earth and dirty foods. Their light disappeared and they could not fly. They could not see their companion gods and goddesses. Then they started to have sexual relations. Generations later they ate meat and blood. They started to become violent and kill each other. That was the beginning of being human. Therefore, countless years ago, our lineage grandfather and grandmother gods, did not eat meat. Generations later, eating meat became a bad habit.

Nowadays, we have bad habits everywhere. Millions and millions of people buy and eat meat. This creates the killing, suffering and torture of millions of animals every day! Indirectly this creates animal hell. Therefore all virtuous buyers, sellers and consumers create the same negative karma or sin. This explanation comes from Shakyamuni Buddha's Lankavatara Sutra and Kalachakra Tantra. In chapter six of the Lankavatara Sutra, the Buddha says:

'Hey, Mahamati, if no one eats meat in any way whatsoever, then no living beings will be killed for its sake.

'Mahamati, innocent living beings are killed for the sake of their value; killing for other reasons is rather rare.'

Furthermore, in the tenth chapter of the Dhammapada (a collection of sayings of the Buddha in verse form and one of the most widely read and best-known Buddhist scriptures) it says:

'All tremble at violence;
all fear death.

Putting oneself in the
place of another,

One should not kill,
nor cause to kill.

All tremble at violence;
life is dear to all.

Putting oneself in
the place of another,

One should not kill,
nor cause to kill!'

Therefore, whoever gives up harming others, having understood this in accordance with the situation set forth, is a virtuous practitioner.

Furthermore, in our ordinary thinking, we believe that when we eat meat, it will make us strong and healthy. But in reality, it indirectly causes the decline of our physical health, mental health, brings many sicknesses such as heart and liver disease, high blood pressure, high cholesterol, breast cancer, diseases of the womb and digestive system.

You become forgetful, less intelligent, overly aggressive and violent. And it destroys our realisations, compassion, perfect wisdom or correct understanding and peaceful mind.

Millions of turkeys, chickens and other animals are being killed every day for food and profit. This problem comes from the fact that nowadays money has big power. Money looks like creator god. Of course, people are over-focused on making money. Money even controls leaders of countries. They think that if they have a lot of money they can do anything.

When people believe in this idea, then they care less about an ethical life and good morality.

They over-focus on money, which results in killing, stealing, cheating, lying, destroying the natural environment, the killing of animals and the selling of meat. This reality is a foolish idea because it results in our poor health and brings many sicknesses. It destroys our welfare.

This is my opinion. Please don't believe this immediately. We will continually need to

Photo credit: EFDA

analyse, and come to a real understanding ourselves.

The Buddha as well as the Lankavatara Sutra says:

'Hey, Mahamati, moreover, in this regard those who kill, kill and trade because they want profit.

'Whatever fools eat meat, buy the meat for money. Those who perform the killing want profit, so they kill animals that fly in the sky, live in the water, or walk on the Earth, in many different ways — with iron hooks, slings, and nets — thus seeking profit.

'Mahamati, as there is no so-called meat that has not been ordered, that is without seeking and without perception, you should not eat meat.'

And so, we need to develop great compassion with correct wisdom. This is everyone's important responsibility.

Geshe Thubten Soepa kindly gave permission for this article, transcribed by Carol Beairsto, to be reproduced.

He has taught at many centres run by the Foundation for the Preservation of the Mahayana Tradition around the world.

We Believe in the 'Conservation of the Heart'

"When you eat, remember the farmer"

– Chinese proverb

Chinese culture is a pool of wealth and wisdom. The idea of harmonious and balanced co-existence between humanity and Nature appears in almost all major schools of Chinese traditions and philosophies. It is also reflected in our 'Chinese Dream' [a term used in China today to describe a set of ideals about national prosperity and the building of a better society].

I am inspired by historical Chinese culture: Confucianism, Buddhism and Daoism — three traditions that reflect notions of harmony from different angles. For instance, both Buddhism and Daoism teach us to be compassionate and to extend our compassion to not just other people, but all that is around us — plants, animals, insects, earth, water and air. This harmonious co-existence is a recognition of Nature's rules. For anyone who upholds this belief, it is natural to be compassionate towards life, reflect this belief in food and to turn this into a habit for life.

It is with this belief in mind that I founded Sinew Corporation in 1999. We promote green agriculture and the manufacture of organic vegetarian products. From the very beginning I ensured that Sinew reflected my compassion towards life, as all lives are Nature's gifts. I tell my employees that we must help nurture lives and foster a harmonious and balanced relationship between humanity and Nature.

We promote an organic, vegetarian diet. We understand it is difficult to change people's diets because everyone has developed their own habits. So we tell them: 'The best doctor treats an illness before it is developed; the average doctor treats an illness as it is about to develop and the worst doctor treats an illness after it has developed.' A healthy diet helps people stay healthy and can prevent illness from developing in the first place.

We also believe that ecology is not just part of Nature's system, but a reflection of humanity's inner world. Ecology and life depend on each other. Therefore to improve the eco-system around us, we need to attune our minds and hearts towards being more positive towards life in general. Sinew vows to clean and beautify our environment. In fact, our motto is 'Clean our homeland, clean our farms, clean our water and clean our energy'. We use only organic fertilisers and we encourage other farm owners to use organic fertilisers too. Most of our power comes from solar energy and we always make the best use of water.

But there is more. We believe in the 'conservation of the heart' — that is, with faith and hard work we can help others

Photo credit: Sinew

Photo credit: Sinew

see the importance of conservation from within. Once they appreciate this, hopefully they will join us in protecting our homeland and our planet. Today, Sinew is one of the most famous organic vegetarian corporations in China. The combined asset of our companies now totals more than £200 million ($321 million), with an annual output value of £50 million ($80.4 million).

The farm is located in Caijiawa village, in Beijing's Miyun County, about a 90-minute drive from Beijing's urban centre. It consists of a farming area of 10,000 mu (approximately 1,600 acres) and an industrial area of 400 mu (65 acres). We sell raw produce such as cherries, mushrooms, soybeans, wheat and other vegetables, but a large proportion of our crops is processed on our farm and sold to restaurants and supermarkets. Our products include drinks, bean curd, and bakery products. This means that only the freshest food is delivered and also ensures food safety. We strive to present our model of business as an example to others and we have developed agricultural tourism on our farm. Government officials, farm owners and businessmen visit us and observe our green practices. Our methods

offer them ideas that they can then take home with them. Tourists are also welcome to see the farm, learn about organic farming and enjoy the beautiful natural setting.

'Ethical business' is the standard I believe my corporation embraces. It also reflects the core value that guides Sinew's daily operations. For me, ethical business is a faith, a pride and a responsibility. It is also a choice — of how we live our life and how we choose our life's mission. Facing fierce market competition, some businesses believe they don't have a choice; they can't 'do the right thing' for fear of losing the competitive edge. But we tell them that we can be successful and be ethical at the same time. The story of Sinew proves that with faith, life is not just about breathing. It is a mission — to make this world a better place for all.

Lin Xin, pictured above, founded Sinew Corporation in 1999. She is also the founder of the Special Fund of Food Safety for Youth and Children and is known in China for promoting healthy diets, lifestyles and ecological conservation.

Buddhist Dietary Rules

More than half the world's population live in countries where Buddhism is now, or has been, dominant. Buddhism was founded around 550 BC by Siddhartha Gautama who travelled the Ganges plains teaching the path to enlightenment and became known as the Buddha, or Enlightened One. There are about 500 million Buddhists today, and the vast majority live in South-East Asia. Within the three major traditions or branches of Buddhism, there are hundreds of smaller organisations and groups.

Buddhist dietary practice varies enormously between traditions, but all schools of Buddhism have rituals involving food — offering food, receiving food, eating food. Offering food is one of the oldest Buddhist rituals. The first monks received their food as charity and in countries such as Thailand, monks still rely on alms for most of their meals.

Vegetarianism is widely associated with Buddhists but the Buddha was not a vegetarian and did not teach his disciples to be vegetarians. In fact, if meat were put into a monk's alms bowl, he was supposed to eat it. However, the Buddha banned eating the meat of any animal that was 'seen, heard or suspected' to have been killed specifically for the benefit of monks.

The First Precept of Buddhism is do not kill. And some argue that to eat meat is taking part in killing by proxy. Others are vegetarian as part of their practice of *metta* (loving kindness) towards living animals. Whatever they eat, Buddhists are expected to show moderation and self-control in eating, as well as in other aspects of life. Most Theravada monks eat only once or twice a day. Some believers do not eat onions, garlic, chives, leeks or asafoetida (a strong-smelling spice eaten mainly in India), referring to these as the 'five pungent spices', as they tend to excite the senses.

Photo credit: Wonderlane

Buddhist Festival Food

Laba: The Laba festival is held on the eighth (ba) day of the twelth month (la) in the Chinese lunar calendar and features a special rice pudding, or congee called 'Labazhou'. There are a number of legends associated with this centuries-old dish.

One of them tells that the first Labazhou was made by a poor mother whose ungrateful son drove her to beg food from the neighbours. One gave a handful of grains, another a tray of fruits, a third a bowl of beans, according to The Moon Year, by Juliet Bredon and Igor Mitrophanow.

Buddhists later adopted Labazhou as a remembrance feast for their beloved Kuan Yin (Goddess of Mercy) and eat it in commemoration of the day when she gathered fruits and grains for a last meal under her father's roof before leaving to become a nun.

Another legend says soon after the Buddha became a monk, he collapsed from lack of food. A village girl came across him, and gave him a rice pudding containing nuts and berries from the area. It was after this that the Buddha sat down to meditate under the Bohdi tree (where he became fully awakened).

In China today Labazhou is served to worshippers in Buddhist temples during the Laba festival, and contains at least eight 'treasures' or delicious ingredients. Each region has its own recipe. Some versions look like porridge; this version is a moulded pudding commonly eaten in Hong Kong and southern China.

The ingredients are widely available in Chinese/Asian stores or by ordering online. It's also fine to substitute any you can't find with other grains, seeds and fruits (raisins for jujube, for example).

Eight Treasure Rice

Ingredients

(Use planet friendly, fairly traded, free-range ingredients wherever possible.)

Serves six to eight

For the pudding:

225g / 8oz / three-quarters cup glutinous rice, uncooked

40g / 1 and a half oz lard, butter or vegetable shortening

2 tbsp sugar

15 dried red jujube (Chinese dates)

Handful of raisins

15 dried longans (a tropical fruit from the same family as lychees)

15 lotus seeds

10 walnut halves

10 glacé cherries

10 pieces candied angelica, chopped

225g / 8oz can sweetened chestnut puree or red bean paste

For the syrup:

3 tbsp sugar

300ml / half pint / 10 fl oz cold water

1 tbsp cornflour, blended with 2 tbsp water

Method

Place the rice in a saucepan, cover with water and bring to the boil. Cover and simmer for up to 15 minutes or until the water has been absorbed. Add 25g / 1oz of the lard/butter/shortening and the sugar to the cooked rice. Mix well.

Brush a 900ml / 1 and a half pint mould or pudding basin with the remaining lard/butter/shortening. Cover the bottom and sides with a thin layer of the rice mixture. Gently press a layer of the fruit and nuts into the rice, making a pattern that will show through when the pudding is turned out. Cover the fruit and nuts with a thicker layer of rice. Fill the centre with the chestnut puree or red bean paste. Cover with the remaining rice. Flatten the top. Cover with a pleated circle of greaseproof (waxed) paper and secure with string.

Steam the pudding for one hour. Just before it is ready, make the syrup. Dissolve the sugar in the water and bring to the boil. Stir in the cornflour mixture and simmer gently, stirring until thickened. Turn the pudding out on to a warmed serving plate. Pour over the syrup and serve immediately.

Buddha's Delight

Spring Festival: Buddha's Delight (Luohanzhai) is a Buddhist vegetarian dish that is served to mark Spring Festival, also known as Chinese New Year. It is said that before the Buddha passed away, of all his disciples it was the 18th arhat (a disciple, called a a lohan or luohan in China) that he specifically asked not to reach nirvana in order to stay in this world to preach Buddhist teachings. Many Buddhist temples have statues of the 18th arhat, called called Fuhu Luohan (the disciple who tamed a tiger), for this reason.

Buddha's Delight is served in honour of him and usually includes 18 different vegetables and fruit. This dish is served during Spring Festival as a way to pay respect to the Buddha and his disciples.

Because it can be hard to find all 18 ingredients, the recipe has been adapted many times over the years by chefs and families to make it easier to cook. We offer one of the simplified recipes here. The more expensive and rare ingredients are generally eaten only at this special time of year. Find these ingredients in Chinese/Asian stores or order online.

Ingredients

(Use planet friendly, fairly traded, free-range ingredients wherever possible.)

50g / 2oz bamboo shoots
50g / 2oz lotus root
50g / 2oz straw mushrooms
15g / three-quarters oz dried bean curd sticks
15g / three-quarters oz dried wood ear mushrooms
15g / three-quarters oz dried tiger lily bulbs
10g / half oz dried black moss
4 tbsp oil
1 tsp cornstarch mixed with 1 tbsp cold water
1 tbsp light soy sauce
1 tsp sugar
1 tsp salt
2 tsp sesame oil for garnish

Method

Soak the dried vegetables separately in cold water overnight, or in warm water for at least an hour.

Cut bean curd sticks into short lengths. Cut bamboo and lotus root into small slices.

Place a wok or large frying pan over the heat. When hot, add half the oil and wait until it smokes. Stir-fry all the dry vegetables with a little salt for one minute. Remove vegetables from wok and set aside. Add and heat remaining oil and stir-fry rest of the vegetables with a little salt. Add the partly cooked dried vegetables, sugar, and soy sauce, stirring constantly. If it dries out, add a little water.

When cooked add cornstarch mix. Garnish with sesame oil and serve immediately.

Changing Habits is Uncomfortable and Inconvenient...

"If a man can control his body and mind and thereby refrains from eating animal flesh and wearing animal products, I say he will really be liberated"

— Surangama Sutra

Many traditions encourage people to show compassion to humans but as fellow sentient beings, we should also include animals. In Buddhism animals are, like us, also considered to have the potential for enlightenment and hence we can assist them in meaningful ways to achieve happiness and freedom from suffering.

Enlightenment For The Dear Animals is a project aimed at helping people, particularly Buddhists, to develop a greater understanding of the suffering of animals, our role in that suffering and how we can cause less harm to animals. It supports a number of projects around the world, including two Animal Liberation Sanctuaries in Nepal and India.

The first precept in Buddhism is not to kill; the second is not to steal. If we check, why would it be acceptable to accept something for personal use or gain that has been killed but not accept something that was stolen? It is only through analysis and honest self-reflection that we can challenge some of our habits that are in actuality inconsistent with our core beliefs.

Every day we make choices on what we eat without considering the suffering that makes up our food. By adopting a vegetar-ian, or, even better, vegan lifestyle we can reduce this suffering. Billions of animals are killed around the world every year so that people can eat their flesh. We can make an active choice to lessen our contribution to the killing (and therefore lessen the karma of killing accumulated by others, such as those who work in abattoirs). Even though we are not directly doing the killing, we are still actively contributing to these deaths. According to the Lankavatara Sutra the Buddha said:

'It is not true, Mahamati, that meat is proper food and is permissible for the Sravaka when [the victim] was not killed by himself, when he did not order others to kill it, when it was not specially meant for him.'

The majority of people can lead healthier lives without eating meat, however, they choose not to and say they need to. The saving of animals' lives by resisting the habit for meat does not become a strong motivation until one puts in effort. Changing habits is uncomfortable and inconvenient. However, by using compassion (thinking of how it would be to suffer like those animals) and wisdom (the reality that eating meat is less healthy for us, it leads to environmental impacts, it adds to the cruelty to the world and it creates a distance between us and other beings) and regular reminding, it becomes easier and eventually effortless.

Once you understand how you yourself are contributing to this cruelty, for the compassionate person there is no going back. 'Thus, Mahamati, wherever there is the evolution of living beings, let people cherish the thought of kinship with them, and, thinking that all beings are [to be loved as if they were] an only child, let them refrain from eating meat.'

Tania Duratovic is an ecologist, zoologist and animal welfare consultant.

Phil Hunt is an archaeologist, involved in animal care and rescue.

They are based in Australia.

here are two stories highlighting the work of Enlightenment for the Dear Animals.

saved from the butcher's block

One moment, a billy goat was tied up at one of the many small street butchers' shops in the Kathmandu valley, Nepal, awaiting its turn to be killed and sold as meat.

The next it was rescued by Lama Zopa Rinpoche, a Tibetan Buddhist lama and head of international Buddhist organisation, the Foundation for the Preservation of the Mahayana Tradition, who just happened to be passing the butcher. He sent the goat to join other rescued animals at the Animal Liberation Sanctuary at Kopan Monastery, about 12km north of Kathmandu.

He was called 'Rigzin', meaning 'wise one' in Tibetan, and soon became the leader of the flock of rescued goats and sheep despite not being the oldest, biggest, tallest or fastest. According to Phil Hunt of Enlightenment For The Dear Animals, Rizgin has one of the longest beards and loves being scratched along his cheeks and neck. Phil adds: 'Although he uses his power and strength when necessary to keep the others in line, he also demonstrates concern for those who may be struggling. With a flock now of 35 goats and two sheep, a wise leader is a definite help in managing these very lucky, but still quite cheeky, sentient beings!'

Continued overleaf

the great escape

In Lower Dharamsala, in the Indian Himalayas, there is a yard, like so many others around the world, where the nervous animals that come in have only one fate — a frightening and painful death.

Yet on this morning three slightly nervous Buddhists were let in because they were planning to save three of the condemned. They couldn't choose who would live and die, so they asked the workers to do so. The three sheep shivered, straining at their rope leads as they were pulled away from the rest of their companions.

One of the problems with animals is that you just can't explain things to them easily. The three escapees from death struggled against their rescuers and as their fear and terror grew, they became incapable of walking. So they were carried to safety. These warm, soft, lanolin-greasy bodies, breathing hard but too nervous and weak to struggle further, were a privilege to carry even as their little bodies became heavier and heavier with every step.

Finally, they came to the house of Buddhist teacher (and ex-monk, ex-hippie) Jimi Neal, pictured below with Tania Duratovic, where they were allowed to eat the grass, given special blessings, and later taken to join a flock that an Indian friend of Jimi's looks after, that includes other lifetime rescues.

The rescue was dedicated to the long lives of three precious teachers, including His Holiness the Dalai Lama.

Photo credit: EFDA

What Do Pilgrims Eat?

"It is no use walking anywhere to preach unless our walking is our preaching"

– St Francis of Assisi

In 2007 the 17th Gyalwang Karmapa, spiritual leader to more than one million Himalayan Buddhists, officially turned vegetarian during an annual pilgrimage. And he asked his monks to do the same.

'At first when His Holiness said, "Don't eat meat", the monks thought; "What do you mean?"' said 33-year-old monk Karma Gyaltsen Sonam, from Rumtek monastery, in the Indian state of Sikkim near the capital Gangtok, as he tucked into a cheese pizza. 'But in 2007 at the Kagyu Monlam [an annual pilgrimage to Bodhgaya in India, where the Buddha achieved enlightenment] he asked about 1,000 monks how many of them wanted to take the vow, and they all said yes.'

Since then, all the monks in the Karmapa's monasteries, as well as increasing numbers of his followers, have become vegetarian or most-ly vegetarian, despite the fact that Tibetans and people of the high Himalayan plateau are traditionally huge meat eaters. At those altitudes, and with those barren landscapes, meat has always been the most available food.

There are plenty of ecological reasons for vegetarianism, and the Karmapa has been a champion of the environment since he was a small boy growing up in Tibet as a reincarnate lama. But he made his decision about food for reasons of compassion. Every day many Buddhists say a prayer to 'all sentient beings' and the Karmapa felt that by giving up meat it would help him and his followers remember that the daily prayer includes ALL sentient beings.

Every year there are more than 200 million pilgrimages undertaken all around the world. It is an important part of every major religion that we should take time out of our ordinary life to travel and pray in a different landscape, in order to understand our own inner landscape better.

In 2011 the Alliance of Religions and Conservation launched a Green Pilgrimage Network in the Italian town of Assisi, birthplace of St Francis, Christian saint of animals, and a pilgrim destination for thousands of people every year. The initiative arose from the observation that our holiest cities and places should be the cleanest, purest places, because they are the most loved. And yet (partly because of the pilgrims) these places are actually sometimes the dirtiest and least ecological — or even 'faithful'.

Great Idea!

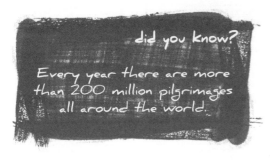

did you know?

Every year there are more than 200 million pilgrimages all around the world.

But what if pilgrimage places announced themselves to be 'green pilgrimage' places? What difference would that make to how the municipal governments galvanised themselves to protect the local environment? What difference would it make to how the faith leaders guided people to behave? And to how pilgrims acted both during their journey and later when they returned home?

Several pilgrimage places have started by surveying their transport, pollution, waste collection, water supply, buildings (old and new), hotels, education, volunteering, pilgrim experience…and food sourcing.

Some faiths already have a strong awareness of how pilgrims should eat simply. 'The worst container to be filled to its utmost capacity is the stomach,' said the Prophet Muhammad in the 7th century. 'It is enough for people to eat what will suffice to keep them standing, but if that is not attainable, then one third for food, one third for drink, and one third empty for air.'

Other religions are rediscovering old traditions. In medieval Christianity, for example, it was normal for pilgrims to eat no meat as they walked to Canterbury, Trondheim, Rome, Jerusalem or Santiago de Compostela. Instead, they would eat vegetables and grains, and fish where it was available. Several pilgrim places are looking at how to revive those ideas in a modern context. So in Etchmiadzin, the headquarters of the Armenian Apostolic Church, people are using simple, sustainable ingredients and old family recipes to give to pilgrims, while reviving a local sense of pride in their traditional slow-cooked, simple food which is so often challenged by the arrival of fast food cultures.

In the rapidly expanding pilgrim city of Louguan in central China, Daoist leaders have set up organic farms, to teach local people and pilgrims about sustainable agriculture. And the Lutheran Church of Norway, as well as the municipality of the pilgrim city of Trondheim, has started to encourage hostels, restaurants and cafés along the pilgrimage routes to Trondheim to be greener, through supporting the well-established Eco-Lighthouse (Miljøfyrtårn) accreditation.

The hope is that today's modern pilgrims will take time as they walk and travel to think about food, to make sure it is kind to animals, the environment and to themselves. And when they go home from this extraordinary experience, some will make changes in how they or their school, business or faith community buys and eats food. And a few will, like the Karmapa, make changes that will influence vast numbers of other people to think more deeply about what 'good' food really is and can be.

Victoria Finlay is Communications Director at the Alliance of Religions and Conservation (ARC)

Epilogue:
Buddhist
Grace

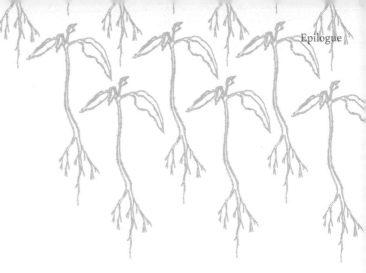

This food is the gift of the whole universe,

Each morsel is a sacrifice of life,

May I be worthy to receive it.

May the energy in this food,

Give me the strength,

To transform my unwholesome
qualities into wholesome ones.

I am grateful for this food,

May I realise the Path of Awakening,

For the sake of all beings.

Namo Amida Buddha.

Useful Websites

Here is a small list of websites you may find helpful. Some of them belong to organisations mentioned in this book; others offer help and inspiration.

A World of Green Muslims: website reporting on Muslim environmental action from around the world: aworldofgreenmuslims.wordpress.com

Ahimsa Dairy Foundation: a British not-for-profit company that provides slaughter-free milk, inspired by the farm at Bhaktivedanta Manor: ahimsamilk.org

AKVO: an international non-profit foundation that builds open source internet and mobile software used to make international development co-operation and aid activity more transparent: akvo.org

Alliance of Religions and Conservation: an international charity working with the world's major faiths to help them develop environmental projects based on their beliefs: arcworld.org

Aqua4all: a Dutch foundation dedicated to improving water and sanitation for the poorest people in the world: aquaforall.nl

Bhaktivedanta Manor: a British International Society of Krishna Consciousness temple, college and farm, which produces Ahimsa milk: bhaktivedantamanor.co.uk

Bhumi Project: an international Hindu environmental programme: bhumiproject.org

CAFOD: the official Catholic aid agency for England and Wales: cafod.org.uk

Care of Creation Kenya: a Kenyan NGO working to mobilise the church in Kenya to respond to serious environmental challenges: kenya.careofcreation.net

Catholic Coalition on Climate Change: US-based campaign to promote the Catholic Church's efforts to embrace an ethic of environmental stewardship: catholicclimatecovenant.org

Chiot's Run: An American organic farm blog: chiotsrun.com

Christian Ecology Link: a UK charity introducing the Earth to the Church, and the Church to the Earth: greenchristian.org.uk

Coalition on the Environment and Jewish Life: works to deepen Jewish commitment to stewardship and protection of the Earth: coejl.org

Compassion in World Farming: the leading farm animal welfare charity that campaigns to end the factory farming of animals and long-distance transport: ciwf.org.uk

Creation Justice Ministries: works with Protestant and Orthodox faith groups, to protect and restore God's Creation. Has a Faithful Harvest Campaign on food and farming: creationjustice.org

Eating Better: For a Fair, Green, Healthy Future: an alliance helping people to eat less meat and the creation of sustainable food and

farming systems: **eating-better.org**

EcoJesuit: international forum connecting Jesuits, people and ecology worldwide, offering reflection and communication on a wide range of faith and environmental issues: **ecojesuit.com**

Ecological Management Foundation: Dutch charity dedicated to improving access to clean drinking water and sanitation facilities in developing countries: **emf.nl**

EcoSikh: an international Sikh environmental programme: **ecosikh.org**

Enlightenment For The Dear Animals: a project aimed at helping people, particularly Buddhists, to help animals: **enlightenmentforanimals.org**

Enough Food For Everyone If: an international campaign against global hunger: **enoughfoodif.org**

Environmental Working Group: American environmental organisation (ewg.org) with an excellent guide on reducing meat-eating: **ewg.org/meateatersguide**

European Christian Environmental Network: a faith network promoting caring for creation: **ecen.org**

Evangelical Environmental Network: a US-based coalition of 23 evangelical Christian programmes dedicated to the care of God's creation: **creationcare.org**

Fairtrade Foundation: a development organisation committed to tackling poverty and injustice through trade: **fairtrade.org.uk**

FareShare: a British charity working to relieve food poverty: **fareshare.org.uk**

Feeding the 5000: a global campaign against food waste: **feeding5k.org**

FishOnline: the Marine Conservation Society's in-depth guide to a wide range of fish and fisheries and their relative sustainability: **fishonline.org**

Food Cycle: a British charity working to alleviate food poverty and social isolation: **foodcycle.org.uk**

Food For Life Partnership: a Soil Association initiative to create a network of schools committed to transforming food culture: **foodforlife.org.uk**

Friends House: the Quakers' headquarters in London, Britain, with environmentally-friendly meeting rooms, conference centre and cafe: **friendshouse.co.uk**

Global One 2015: the international wing of the Faith Regen Foundation (FRF), a Muslim led and multi-faith inspired UK-based charity: **globalone2015.org**

Green Christian: the website of Christian Ecology Link: **greenchristian.org.uk**

Green Deen South Africa: campaign to raise awareness and mobilise action in the South African Muslim community about environmental issues: **greendeen.msa.org.za**

GreenFaith: US-based organisation dedicated to mobilising people of diverse religious backgrounds for environmental leadership. Has produced Repairing Eden, a guide to sustainable food for religious institutions: **greenfaith.org**

Green Gardener: a British company that advises gardeners on green practices: **greengardener.co.uk**

Green Muslims: an American organisation that serves as a bridge between Muslim communities and environmental organisations: **greenmuslims.org**

Greenpeace: an international charity that protects and conserves the environment: greenpeace.org.uk, greenpeace.org

Green Prophet: a sustainable voice for green news on the Middle East region: greenprophet.com

Guerrilla Gardening: a British blog for those wishing to grow food and flowers on neglected land: guerillagardening.org

Hazon: American non-profit organisation working to create healthier and more sustainable communities in the Jewish world, has a food guide on ethical eating for Jews: hazon.org

Interfaith Sustainable Food Collaborative: American network working to reconnect religious people to a sustainable food system through their faith community: interfaithfood.org

Interfaith Power & Light: a US-based religious response to global warming: interfaithpowerandlight.org

International Society for Ecology and Culture: non-profit organisation dedicated to revitalising cultural and biological diversity, and strengthening local communities worldwide: localfutures.org

Landshare: a British movement to connect people with land with others who need it for food cultivation: landshare.net

Love Food Hate Waste: a British movement that raises awareness of the need to reduce food waste: lovefoodhatewaste.com

Lutheran World Federation: a global communion of national and regional Lutheran churches: lutheranworld.org

Lutherans Restoring Creation: initiative designed to encourage the Evangelical Lutheran Church in America (ELCA) to incorporate care for creation into all levels: lutheransrestoringcreation.org

MADE In Europe: A Muslim-led group campaigning against global poverty and injustice: madeineurope.org.uk

Marine Conservation Society: a charity that works for the protection seas, shores and wildlife: mcsuk.org

Marine Stewardship Council: the world's leading certification and eco-labelling programme for sustainable seafood: msc.org

Maryknoll Sisters, New York, USA: maryknollsisters.org

Micro Water Facility (MWF): a Dutch non-profit initiative working to improve access to clean drinking water and proper sanitation in Africa and Asia: microwaterfacility.org

MOA Nature Farming and Culture Foundation: a Japanese organisation that promotes sustainable agriculture which it calls nature farming: moainternational.or.jp

Monastère de Solan, France: monasteredesolan.com

National Religious Partnership for the Environment: US–based association of independent faith groups dedicated to environmental sustainability and justice: nrpe.org

Navdanya: a national movement in India working to protect the diversity and integrity of living resources, especially native seed: navdanya.org

Netiya: a Jewish network with interfaith partners that promotes urban agriculture, creating food gardens on unused institutional

land in Los Angeles: netiya.org

Oxfam: international charity working in development. Has a major focus on food and farming and produced *Growing a Better Future: Food justice in a resource-constrained world*: oxfam.org.uk, oxfam.org

Rain Harvesting Implementation Network: a Dutch organisation helping people implement rainwater harvesting systems around the world: rainfoundation.org

Ready Steady Slow: a Church of England initiative to inspire people to slow down during Advent: readysteadyslow.org

RHS Urban Greening: The Royal Horticultural Society's tips for gardening in towns and cities: rhs.org.uk/gardening/sustainable-gardening/urban-greening

Shrinking the Footprint: the Church of England's national environmental campaign: churchcare.co.uk/shrinking-the-footprint

Sisters of St Francis of Sylvania, Ohio, USA: sistersosf.org

The Simple Way: an inner-city faith community based in Philadelphia, Pennsylvania, USA, that has helped create and connect radical faith communities around the world: thesimpleway.org

Slow Food Movement: a global organisation that links the pleasure of food with a commitment to community and the environment: slowfood.org.uk, slowfood.com

Soil Association: a British charity campaigning for healthy, humane and sustainable food, farming and land use: soilassociation.org

Southern African Faith Communities' Environment Institute: a coalition of communities of different faiths in southern African countries united to care for people and planet: safcei.org

Sustain: the alliance for better food and farming: a British charity advocating food and agriculture policies that enhance the health and welfare of people, animals and the environment: sustainweb.org

Sustainable Food Trust: a British charity exploring solutions for a food-producing system that causes the least harm to humans and the environment: sustainablefoodtrust.org

Tri-State Coalition for Responsible Investment: an alliance of Roman Catholic institutional investors in the New York metropolitan area, USA: tricri.org

WaterAid: an international charity that works to bring safe water and sanitation to the world's poorest communities: wateraid.org

Web of Creation: resources for faith communities: webofcreation.org

The Wesley: the first ethical hotel in Britain, owned and run by Methodists: thewesley.co.uk

Willowbrook Organic Farm: The first organic halal farm in Britain run by the Radwan family: www.willowbrookorganic.org

WWOOF UK: a British charity teaching about organic growing and low-impact lifestyles: wwoof.org.uk

Picture Credits

Page No.	Credit	Page No.	Credit
1	Annie Bungeroth	81	WaterAid
4	Helen Browning	88–89	ARC
4	Kevin Van Bree	92	The Simple Way
8	Sustainable Food Trust	96	Prayudi Hartono
10	ARC	100	Sisters of St Francis of Sylvania, Ohio
13	ARC	103	MOA
14	Redgie Collins	104	ChiotsRun.com
17	Meena Kadri	108	ARC/Richard Stonehouse
19	Methodist Church in Kenya	111	ARC
20	ARC	112–113	Hazon
22–23	Meena Kadri	116	Hazon
26	Pip Campbell-Clause	124	New Roots
31	Jody Morris O'Reilly	126	Hazon
37	Kevin Rawlings	130–131	Tambako the Jaguar
46–47	Partha Sarathi Sahana	133	Preston Rhea
49	Astrid Schulz	137	Ruby Radwan
50	ARC	139	ARC
58	Astrid Schulz	140	ARC
62–63	ChiotsRun.com	146	ARC
65	ARC	148	ARC
70	ARC	152–153	CIWF/Amit Pasricha
77	Soil Association	155	Compassion in World Farming
79	ARC	158	Compassion in World Farming

Page No.	Credit
166	ARC
168	Wonderlane
173	ARC
176-177	ARC
179	Meena Kadri
180	ARC
182	Manfred Uhde
186	ARC
188	Simon Rawles
191	Matthew Jellings
193	Wade Sisler
198-199	Sarah Jamerson
201	Meena Kadri
202	ARC
207	EcoSikh
208	EcoSikh
213-214	Monks Community Forest, Cambodia
216	EFDA
218	Sinew
218	Sinew
219	Wonderlane
225	EFDA
228	Wonderlane

The Alliance of Religions and Conservation (ARC) was founded in 1995 by HRH The Duke of Edinburgh. Its mission is to help major religions around the world develop and carry out their own individual environmental programmes, because — in different ways — their central teachings, beliefs and practices all have nature at their core. ARC also works with key environmental organisations to help them link with religions, creating powerful alliances between faith communities and conservation groups.

Faith in Food is an ARC initiative that builds upon the social and agricultural programmes of the faiths wordwide. It is also aimed at engaging the moral leadership, purchasing power, investment portfolios and land ownership of the world's foremost religions in order to help people rediscover 'a right relationship' with their food and the land it comes from. It is about helping people of faith honour their values in the food they eat, grow and buy.

www.arcworld.org

Faith in Food has been developed with the support of the Royal Norwegian Ministry of Foreign Affairs.

Discover more great titles at

www.bene-factum.co.uk